The Birthplace of Jesus Is in Palestine

The Birthplace of Jesus Is in Palestine

A Memoir

TOINE VAN TEEFFELEN

Foreword by MARIE DENNIS

RESOURCE *Publications* · Eugene, Oregon

THE BIRTHPLACE OF JESUS IS IN PALESTINE
A Memoir

Copyright © 2024 Toine van Teeffelen. All rights reserved. Except for brief quotations in critical publications or reviews, no part of this book may be reproduced in any manner without prior written permission from the publisher. Write: Permissions, Wipf and Stock Publishers, 199 W. 8th Ave., Suite 3, Eugene, OR 97401.

Resource Publications
An Imprint of Wipf and Stock Publishers
199 W. 8th Ave., Suite 3
Eugene, OR 97401

www.wipfandstock.com

PAPERBACK ISBN: 979-8-3852-0724-4
HARDCOVER ISBN: 979-8-3852-0725-1
EBOOK ISBN: 979-8-3852-0726-8

The following copyrighted passages are originally from Van Teeffelen, Toine. *Dagboek Bethlehem 2000–2004*. Nijmegen: De Stiel, 2004:

- 7–11: Bethlehem tussen dorp and stad.
- 13: Proloog: Kerstbrief aan mijn ongeboren kind/
- 26-7: "Van een winkelier (. . .)" until "(. . .) angst en verdriet."
- 30-2: "Zijn echte naam is (. . .)" until "(. . .) schoolkinderen en toeristen."
- 44-5: "Ik spreek een oude kennis (. . .)" until "(. . .) met deze weg geassocieerd."
- 62: "Een zeventienjarig meisje (. . .)" until "(. . .) groen was als gras."
- 73: "Dus werd er geacteerd (. . .)" until "(. . .) de passagiers in lachen uit."
- 77-81: "Op een warme middag slenter (. . .)" until "(. . .) of als in een droom."
- 86-7: "Het is vroeg in de ochtend (. . .)" until "(. . .) zolang de bezetting duurt."
- 90-1: "Als ik thuis ben (. . .)" until "(. . .) alles wat er gebeurd is?"
- 92-3: "Sommige spelletjes van Jara (. . .)" until "(. . .) als een eeuwigheid voorkwamen, liep ze door."
- 94: "Mijn collega Elias vertelt (. . .)" until "(. . .) het leven houden."
- 95: "De voornaamste gebeurtenissen (. . .)" until "(. . .) Jara er in paniek raakt."
- 96: "Vrijdag stierf een man (. . .)" until "(. . .) zegt Janet."
- 97: "Veel mensen voelen zich (. . .)" until "(. . .) kijkt naar het zonlicht."
- 98-101: "Meer dan drie weken uitgaansverbod (. . .)" until "(. . .) wanneer ze uit het zicht van buitenlanders zijn."
- 101-2: "Jara en ik spelen (. . .)" until "(. . .) op haar borst drukt."
- 104-5: "Iedere keer nog is de hoop (. . .)" until "(. . .) precies het tegenovergestelde?"

- 108-9: "Een docent zei droogjes (. . .)" until "(. . .) of het een tank was."
- 109-10: "Jara zei dat ze gedroomd had (. . .)" until "(. . .) ver weg, uitgezet."
- 110: "Ze vraagt leerlingen (. . .)" until "(. . .) van God kon komen."
- 112: "Wanneer buurman Brahim Jara (. . .)" until "(. . .) een liedje dat Jara graag zingt."
- 114-5: "Misschien is 'krokodil' toch niet (. . .)" until "(. . .) in de gaten houden."
- 116: "Deze avond hoor ik (. . .)" until "(. . .) is om half drie."
- 118: "Op terugweg naar Bethlehem (. . .)" until "(. . .) denk ik bij mezelf."
- 120: "Jara zegt dat het genoeg is zo." Until "(. . .) zij geeft niet op."
- 125-6: "Mary en ik waren (. . .)" until "(. . .) we leven nog!"
- 127-8: "Op 28 maart (. . .)" until "(. . .) Waar waren Christine's engelen?"
- 132-4: "Ismail, het schoolhoofd (. . .)" until "(. . .) meer dan anderhalf uur."
- 148: "Ons huis ligt in de nabijheid (. . .)" until "(. . .) het landschap mag ademen."

Publishing House De Stiel gave permission to use these passages in the present book and its electronic version.

With Mary, Jara and Tamer

Contents

Foreword | xi

Acknowledgements | xv

1. The Village, a City | 1
2. Housebound | 14
3. A Land of Testing | 32
4. The Mad Permit Game | 45
5. Rhythms of Life | 62
6. The Gift of Home | 70
7. The Past in the Present | 79
8. Good Morning, Dignity | 94
9. Challenging the Wall | 100
10. Hiking the Land | 112
11. Reclaiming Beauty | 127
12. A Resilient Presence | 136
13. The Hellish Road | 146
14. Common Home | 153
15. Sumud and Hope | 157

Afterword: Bethlehem, Christmas 2023 | 163

Recommended Reading | 167

Bibliography | 169

Foreword

DURING MULTIPLE VISITS TO Palestine and Israel over the past twenty-five years, my time with author Toine van Teeffelen and others at the Arab Education Institute (AEI), an organizational member of Pax Christi International, has been the highlight—a privileged opportunity to hear Palestinian stories and to witness the challenge of Palestinian life under occupation. Women, in particular, who gathered in what became the Sumud Story House at AEI, shared the richness of their cultural values and practices and the iniquity of dehumanization and violence that they encountered day after day.

As the massive Separation Wall increasingly dominated life in Bethlehem where AEI is located, the Wall became a focus of remarkable creativity and clear, nonviolent resistance. Concerts and games at the base of the Wall helped Palestinians imagine gliding over that enormous structure. Eventually the Wall Museum began to take shape. Described well here in chapter 6: *Challenging the Wall*, the Wall Museum made the history of Palestine, the experience of Palestinians and solidarity messages from around the world permanently visible.

Founded in 1945 after the Second World War, Pax Christi International (PCI), with whom I most often travelled to Palestine, is a Catholic peace movement with a long history of accompanying and supporting a global network of grassroots organizations like AEI as they seek just peace using nonviolent means in their own contexts.

About 15 years ago Pax Christi began to collect stories about the methodology and impact, success or failure, faith-connection or not of nonviolent practices from different, often very violent, contexts where Pax Christi members live or work. The movement began to see creativity, wisdom and, frequently, the power and effectiveness of nonviolent strategies from Colombia to Lebanon, Syria to Sudan, Guatemala to the Philippines and beyond, despite the fact that nonviolent options were often dismissed as passive, naïve, even irresponsible in the "real" world.

PCI recognizes that the understanding and practice of nonviolence will be different in different contexts—challenged and shaped by the history and contemporary experience of those on the receiving end of violence, That is powerfully evident in Palestine for example, where dehumanizing occupation, children killed and imprisoned, demolished houses and olive groves, economic and cultural violence, military attacks and, now, a war of immense brutality could make nonviolence seem completely irrelevant in this difficult twenty-first century.

As an international movement, our commitment is to a nonviolence that is not just *not violent* but is actively engaged in interrupting violence of whatever kind. We have learned much from what appears to be a strong Palestinian commitment to nonviolence as a way of life and a collection of creative strategies for ending the occupation and achieving just peace. We are also encouraged by the empirical research of scholars like Erica Chenoweth and Maria Stephan, demonstrating that nonviolent campaigns for liberation and justice can be significantly more effective than violent uprisings.

But it is also clear that decisions about whether and when to use nonviolent strategies must be made by those most affected by the violence. who also pay the high cost of nonviolent action. Examples abound in Palestine—from the strategic nonviolence of the first intifada to the vision of Kairos Palestine, from the Boycott, Divestment and Sanctions (BDS) movement to the Great March of Return in 2018 and 2019.

Palestinians, Israelis and their allies have for years been trying to build just peace and claim a dignified life for all people in the Holy Land using nonviolent tools. Numerous nonviolent campaigns led by Palestinians since the late 1980s have resisted the occupation and sought a way forward toward peace, while several peace movements and organizations in Israel have also been calling for a nonviolent solution to this decades-long conflict. On the West Bank, Israelis who oppose the occupation have joined Palestinians to provide a protective presence in Bedouin villages, while international allies have been accompanying children to school in Hebron, communities facing demolition in East Jerusalem and struggles over land and water in the Jordan Valley.

In February 2023, I participated in the most recent Pax Christi International delegation to the Holy Land in an effort to understand the

FOREWORD

increasing violence. Once again we saw the devastating consequences of occupation, the violence of an apartheid system represented by the massive Wall separating families from their land and from each other, children from their schools, people from their olive trees. Despite the dehumanizing brutality, however, the people have stayed—literally if possible, and symbolically. They call their steadfastness sumud, a powerful expression of nonviolent resistance that is the dominant subject of this book.

The obstacles they repeatedly meet are formidable: trauma, fear, dehumanization, violence, corruption, and all the physical and psychological violences of the occupation.

For decades, day by day, Toine van Teeffelen has experienced life under occupation. His memoir captures the beauty, the struggle and the heartbreak of that long experience. His "Afterword," written in the midst of the Israeli war in Gaza that reached an unconscionable level of violence after the Hamas attack in Israel on 7 October 2023, raises even more challenging questions about the efficacy of nonviolence, including sumud, in the context of such brutal violence against civilians whose resilience and fundamental commitment to nonviolence are legendary but finite.

Toine writes, "The meaning of sumud, as well as comparable concepts like resilience, hope or resistance, can become hollow and perverted when they create impossible demands while taking away other people's responsibility to fight for a change in the overall inhuman situation such as in Gaza."

The nonviolent steps that could still be taken are increasingly difficult, but violence, even defensive violence, has, until now, led to a dead end—literally. This book should inspire the world to join the Palestinians' nonviolent struggle for an end to the occupation, a dignified life and genuine security for every Palestinian and every Israeli. It offers an inspired understanding of the power of sumud in the context of enduring brutality.

Marie Dennis
Senior Director, Catholic Nonviolence Initiative
Pax Christi International

Acknowledgements

My heartfelt gratitude goes out to the individuals and organizations whose contributions played an important role in the development and realization of this book:

- Abdelfatah Abu Srour, Nora Carmi, Adnan Musallem, Walid Mustafa, the late Salah Ta'amari, and Zoughby Zoughby, for generously sharing insights into the development, various meanings, and applications of sumud.
- Colleagues at AEI in Bethlehem: Fuad Giacaman, Rania Murra, Elias Abu Akleh, Roger Salameh, Claudette Salameh, and Sahar Fakhouri, for their invaluable engagement with the various projects mentioned in the book.
- Susan Atallah, for generously providing numerous stories as well as corrections of inaccuracies.
- Wim Bartels for his consistent encouragement of peace movement-related work in Palestine over the years.
- Gied ten Berge, for insightful discussions on the challenges of the peace movement worldwide and the profound meanings of pilgrimage to Bethlehem and Palestine.
- Fr Peter Bonneville DuBrul, for sharing critical theories and theological insights.
- Riet Bons, for years of encouragement for peace and justice efforts in Palestine and the Netherlands.
- Teun van Dijk, for sensitizing me to the discourse dimensions of language.
- Meta Floor, for her perspectives on solidarity.

Acknowledgements

- The members of the Friends of Young Bethlehem in the Netherlands, especially my brother Paul van Teeffelen, whose close support over the years was invaluable, as well as Sjaak Kuijer, Wini Zaaijer, Ada Krowinkel, Lidy Meier, and Jaap Groeneveld for their support and encouragement to help developing projects for Palestinian youth.
- Thom Geurts, for engaging conversations on sumud, education, and Dutch-Palestinian school exchanges.
- Mary Grey, for many exchanges on sumud, Palestine and theology.
- The late Jan ter Laak, for encouraging my work in the Dutch peace movement Pax Christi.
- Sharif Kanaana, for bringing over his love for folk stories and folk practices of Palestine.
- Pax Christi and its various sections, for their support in AEI's non-violent and creative peace activism, contributions to the World Week for Peace in Palestine Israel, and their assistance in spreading the blogs out of which this book is composed. Special thanks to Pat Gaffney and Ann Farr.
- Anneke van der Putte of Publishing House De Stiel, who was the first to encourage and facilitate the publication of the diaries written during the second Intifada.
- Alexandra Rijke, for collaborative research and exchanges on sumud.
- Rosemary Sayigh, for encouraging the publication of diary entries or blogs written over the years.
- Solidariteitsfonds in Zwolle (Netherlands), for broadening the possibilities of disseminating this book.

A thank you also to Publishing House De Stiel in Nijmegen (Netherlands) for giving permission to take over passages from my Dutch-language book: *Dagboek Bethlehem 2000-2004*. Nijmegen: De Stiel, 2004.

A thank you furthermore to Publishing House Narratio in Gorinchem (Netherlands) for allowing to take over previous passages for this book which appeared in: *Liefde, Woede en Waardigheid: Leven als Gezin op de Bezette Westelijke Jordaanoever*. [Love, Anger and Dignity: Living as Family in the Occupied West Bank]. Gorinchem: Narratio, 2014.

Acknowledgements

I am grateful to UK aid organization CAFOD for allowing the use of the interview with Faten from Artas, which was originally published on their website.

Several interviews about sumud as well as other passages appeared originally in local publications by the Arab Educational Institute, Bethlehem: Culture and Palestine series. They can be accessed in Arab Educational Institute-Pax Christi, *Sumud Reader* (see Bibliography).

The photos were made by AEI staff, Paul van Teeffelen (checkpoint photo) and Lutheran Church in Bethlehem (final photo, of the manger in the collapsed house). The map was produced by RAI in Beit Jala.

The support and contributions from each of these contributors have been invaluable. I am deeply grateful for their collaboration and encouragement throughout the journey of developing this book.

And finally, a very special thanks to my wife, Mary, and our children, Jara and Tamer, for their enduring love and support over the years, also in together developing and refining the book.

Toine van Teeffelen
December 2023

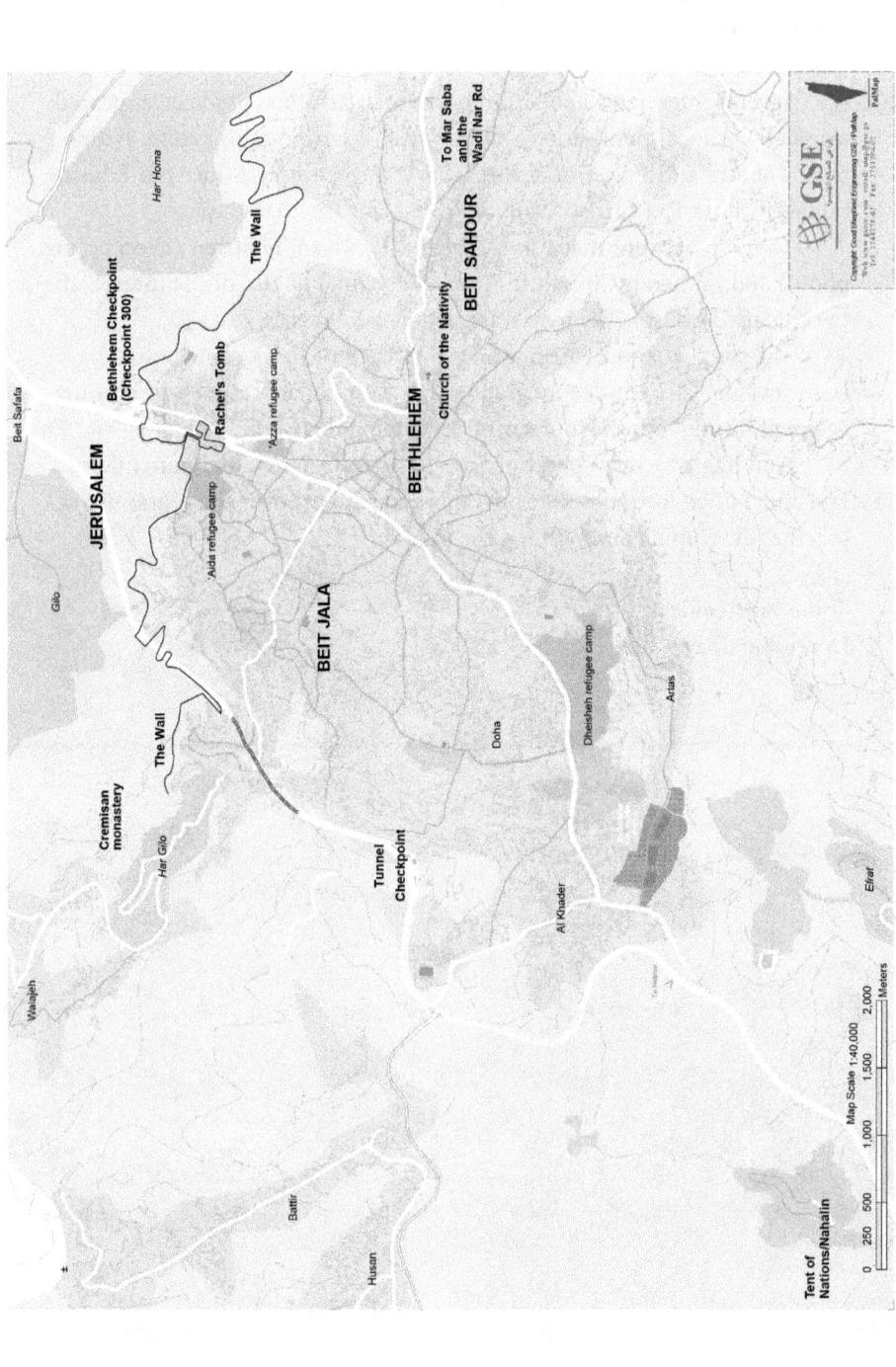

1

The Village, a City

ONCE, A PALESTINIAN TAXI driver playfully remarked upon learning that I resided in Bethlehem, saying, "You must be attending church every day." The name Bethlehem is globally recognized, evoking images of domestic warmth and Christmas carols. To the tourist, Bethlehem appears as a compilation of sacred sites, bringing the Biblical narrative to life. For the avid newspaper reader, Bethlehem is situated in the occupied West Bank, a few kilometers south of Jerusalem. However, for someone like me, who has called it home with my family since 1995, Bethlehem is primarily a community of friendly, welcoming, and open-hearted people, totaling around 35,000 souls.

The identity of Bethlehem is best explained by a paradox. Bethlehem is a Palestinian community with a village-like social structure where many people know each other well. At the same time, it is also, at least in ambition, a city. In the wake of the many visitors who, for hundreds of years, especially after the mid-19th century, came from all directions, Bethlehem acquired urban allure—although those visitors also made an effort to continue seeing the Biblical village, the little town, in it.

It was Bethlehem's intention to propagate this village-urban combination in the project Bethlehem 2000. The year served as a reminder of what happened two millennia ago, but also suggested a jump across a new threshold towards a modern city-like future. Bethlehem would become an engine of the new Palestinian tourist industry. The downtown city was reconstructed, rehabilitated, and repainted in dark green with significant contributions from European and Japanese funds. Exhibitions and music groups came from all over the world; the number of international contacts grew rapidly.

The village–urban duality is rooted in Bethlehem's history. During St Jerome's stay at the end of the fourth century, there were holy masses in many languages in the Church of Nativity. Together with the adjoining monasteries, the church complex was in the following centuries at times larger than the village itself, which remained neglected for a long time. Early in the Turkish period (1516–1920), Christian Arab tribes arrived from Jordan and Yemen to add to the existing Arab population, and western religious immigrants, especially Franciscans, came from Europe to become guardians over the Christian holy places.

Different ethnic groups settled in *haraat* (singular *hara*), clusters of houses built tightly around a courtyard, with small windows like in a castle, so that the extended families were protected in case of outside attacks. When the French and Italians were victorious in the European Crimean War of 1854–5, new Christian orders came to Bethlehem under the protection of European powers. Not without rivalry and with a certain missionary and imperialist drive, they set up their own institutions for education and medical care. New modern building complexes arose around the traditional *haraat* in the following decades. The period of the second half of the nineteenth century was perhaps the clearest moment of transition from a village into the beginnings of a city.

For a long time, Bethlehem remained almost entirely Christian, although a small Muslim *hara* existed since the late 17th century. The demographic situation of Bethlehem changed because of the continuous emigration of Christians. Already at the end of the nineteenth century, Bethlehem Christians sought economic adventures abroad, stimulated by the demand in Catholic Middle and South America for Holy Land products, such as olive wood figurines and mother-of-pearl decorations for which Bethlehem was known. Many Christian Bethlehemites acquired a good knowledge of languages and made international contacts through the Christian missionary schools and institutions established in Jerusalem and Bethlehem. Some of the more adventurous businessmen started to establish export markets in the Catholic Latin-American countries and emigrated. They often did so under the pressure of the deteriorating circumstances in Palestine before and during the First World War when young people tried to escape recruitment into the Turkish army.

The Village, a City

In addition, because of the conflict between the Palestinian inhabitants of the country and the Zionist movement, which stimulated Jewish immigration and land purchases, quite a few people who could afford it left in the first half of the twentieth century. Christians could make use of their foreign contacts, such as emigrated relatives or religious institutions where people had followed education and which had their headquarters in Western countries. The family ties with foreign countries contributed to the character of Bethlehem as an internationally oriented though small-scale community.

As a result of the 1948 Arab-Israeli war, Palestinians from the areas newly called Israel, mostly Muslims but also Christians, fled from their ancestral lands to the surrounding regions, including the West Bank. Three refugee camps were set up in and near Bethlehem by the United Nations. The camps are still there, although they now look like shanty towns. Other refugees from 1948 established themselves in other parts of the town. Perhaps a majority of present-day Bethlehem residents are, in fact, refugees or descendants of refugees.

Bethlehem has many unexpected aspects that can be explained by its complicated history: blue eyes that are sometimes jokingly associated with the Crusader period; Muslims who used to learn the Hosanna in Christian schools; the daily mingling of the bells of the Church of Nativity with the *muezzin*'s call to prayer from the adjacent Mosque of 'Omar; a luxury hotel that borders a refugee camp; a modern international center next to a cobbler's shop from the Turkish era; children of visiting relatives who want to learn Arabic.

There is also that unexpected Middle Eastern combination of identities. The founder and former director of the Arab Educational Institute where I work, Fuad Giacaman, calls himself Palestinian, Arab, resident of Bethlehem, Christian, and Roman-Catholic. All these aspects have meaning for him. His neighbors might form a different combination, especially with regard to religion. His surname "Giacaman" betrays Italian influence. He says he thrives in a Christian-Muslim environment. With his diverse identities, he places himself between east and west, north and south, and calls himself a bridge builder.

For a number of years, Bethlehem served as a meeting point where Palestinians and Israelis would encounter each other in daily life. After the June 1967 war between Israel and the Arab countries, when the West Bank fell under Israeli military rule, the locals held onto the belief for some years that the occupation could be relatively liberal and open. Israelis would come to Bethlehem for the affordability of groceries and restaurants, or to acquire trinkets for creating an Oriental-themed corner in their homes. In the 1970s, Bethlehem's mayor, Elias Freij, attempted to please various parties to maintain Bethlehem's status as a pilgrimage site. Bethlehem generally appeared more tranquil and conservative compared to other more nationalist cities in the West Bank, such as Hebron and Nablus.

However, this sense of calm already underwent significant change before the first Intifada (uprising against the Israeli occupation) in the late 1980s. Despite its reputation for hospitality and openness, Bethlehem found itself gradually encircled by Jewish settlements. Institutions like the university and schools, which were hubs for protests against the occupation, faced closures and other repressive measures.

I settled in Bethlehem in the mid-1990s with my Palestinian-Christian wife, Mary Morcos, whom I had met on a blustery winter day in 1993 at the gates of Bethlehem University. To say we "settled" might not be entirely accurate. Even amidst the Oslo peace process of that era, life on the ground was challenging. The common sentiment among local Palestinians at the time was, "Everything here is difficult." The checkpoint system around Jerusalem was fully enforced, Israeli settlements continued to expand, the division between the West Bank and Gaza was entrenched, and the weight of the oppressive occupation persisted.

For Mary, her connection to Bethlehem ran deep through various threads. It wasn't just because her family resided there and she held a position as a librarian at the university. She embodied the traditional rhythm of the community—unhurried yet unwilling to wait indefinitely. "I take pride in being born in Bethlehem, the birthplace of Jesus, and in giving birth to my children here," she expressed on a TV program shortly after our daughter Jara's birth. She also felt at ease in her role as a hostess and representative of Bethlehem, whether interacting with visiting journalists (who occasionally dropped by to hear how the Morcos family was faring as an "average" Bethlehem family), relatives from Paris, or foreign visitors to her university's Palestiniana library, which later evolved into the Turathuna [our heritage] Center.

Living alongside her, I too found a sense of belonging here—not just due to the warmth of hospitality, but also because of my fascination with living within and observing diverse cultures, fostered by my anthropological background.

Mary's roots in Bethlehem run deep and are intertwined with religious connotations. Her father bears the name Abdallah Morcos, with Abdallah meaning "servant of God." The Morcos family name derives from St Mark, the Gospel writer. The family traces its distant origins back to Yemen, where certain Arab tribes were baptized in the early centuries after Christ. This could possibly be attributed to evangelizing efforts by followers of St Mark, who might have journeyed from Alexandria in Egypt southward to the Arabian Peninsula.

Abdallah Morcos, also known as Abou Hannah (the father of Hannah, a son), was born in 1917, just a few days after the issuance of the Balfour Declaration. In this declaration, the then British Minister of Foreign Affairs promised the Jews a homeland in Palestine under the condition that the rights of what were euphemistically referred to as the "non-Jewish" citizens would not be infringed upon. Abou Hannah's life spanned the entire conflict in Palestine, but he did not live long enough to witness its conclusion.

Although born not in Palestine but in Chile, Abou Hannah was part of a Palestinian family seeking opportunities in the international souvenir trade. During his early years, he grew up in Santiago de Chile. However, he was later brought back to Palestine by his mother and uncle, while his father, for business reasons, remained in Chile where he passed away shortly thereafter.

In the 1930s, Abou Hannah married Emily Salman, a name derived from "Suleiman" or "Solomon." They celebrated their honeymoon in Jericho, near the Jordan River—a winter destination where horse races were a common sight at the time. He was fortunate to find employment in a cafeteria of the British Mandate army, stationed in the southern part of Jerusalem. It was during this time that he developed a lifelong admiration for British organization and discipline. The British era was relatively favorable from an economic standpoint, especially during the 1940s, yet it was politically uncertain due to ongoing clashes between indigenous Arabs and migrating and colonizing Jews. Following 1948, the Jordanian period brought about the opposite scenario—more political stability but economic challenges.

During the Jordanian era, travel was notably easier for Abou Hannah and his family. While present-day West Bank inhabitants often struggle to move in and out of the region, he, his wife, or his brother could freely journey to Damascus and Beirut to purchase fashionable clothing and delectable dried fruits. They could reach Beirut in a day or less. For today's

Palestinian youth, Damascus and Beirut seem far removed, usually only familiar through television or the internet.

Initially, Abou Hannah worked at a grocery store in Bethlehem, earning just a few dinars per month during the 1960s. Later, he collaborated with a Muslim colleague to operate a shop selling spare car parts near Rachel's Tomb—a multi-religious holy site in the northern part of Bethlehem. Adjacent to his shop was a Jewish café frequented by passing travelers. Following the 1967 war, his son Hannah departed for France, and once established there, his sisters Norma and Rita followed suit.

Like countless other families in Bethlehem, the Morcos family lives with one foot in the East and the other in the West. This duality isn't solely physical but also extends to their mindset. In the family's conversations, I discern an ongoing East-West dialogue. Perhaps it's no coincidence that many Christian Palestinians are engaged in communicative professions. For instance, Hannah once served as the director of the Arabic section at Radio Monte Carlo in Paris—a significant radio station in the Middle East at the time. Norma is a film director whose works, including "The Veiled Hope," a documentary about Palestinian women, have circulated at film festivals. Rita previously worked as an Arabic-French teacher. Mary, my wife, serves as a librarian and curator at Bethlehem University's heritage center, catering to university students, school children, and international visitors alike.

Mary's recollections of her childhood in Bethlehem are relatively carefree:

> We lived in Wadi Ma'aleh, not far from the Church of the Nativity. We had a good piece of land around the house and its courtyard, with fig and pomegranate trees, as well as cactuses. The figs were incredibly delicious! I spent time playing with my cousins outdoors, climbing trees for fun, and engaging in children's games. We even had a sheep, along with two mischievous roosters that used to attack people. Some family members were even afraid to step outside the room. When we had water shortages, my sisters would walk a few hundred meters to the nearby well, carrying large buckets.
>
> My family owned a parcel of land not far from the Frères (De la Salle) School. Olive picking there took several days. The entire family participated in the harvest, along with some hired workers. The adults did the tough work—the men climbed ladders into the trees, while the women collected olives on large pieces of rough cloth. A donkey carried the olives, and after extracting the oil,

we would spread them out to dry on the roof of our house. My grandmother, who lived with us, prepared rice, lentils, and salad for the daily lunch during the harvest. Alongside playing with my cousins, the olive harvest remains one of my happiest childhood memories.

At that time, local traveling was easy, unlike today. On Sundays, we often went with our father and uncles to watch horse races in Jericho. We would bring food with us. Another activity was going to the two cinemas in Bethlehem. One ticket would grant admission to two films—they screened Arabic, Indian, and karate movies.

Regarding the Israeli presence during the occupation, after the 1967 June War, Israeli soldiers were commonly seen on the streets. Administrative tasks became notably challenging with the Israeli army involved—tasks such as obtaining identity documents or dealing with travel matters. Humiliation was commonplace, and people sometimes couldn't even access their own offices. Now, of course, it's even worse as they continue to take over land. My uncle owned large stretches of land north of Bethlehem, filled with olive trees, near the former Abu Ghneim forest, now the settlement of Har Homa. During a protest against the expropriation, he was physically removed from his land by an Israeli bulldozer. Other family members also lost their lands in that area.

When Mary and I got married in 1995, there was a brief sense of liberation following the conclusion of the Oslo Accords and the establishment of Palestinian autonomy. At that time, she and her family celebrated by driving through the city in a convoy of cars with horns blaring. However, skepticism and disappointment soon set in. The occupation persisted amidst pockets of Palestinian autonomy. Domestic travel problems worsened due to new checkpoints between Bethlehem and Jerusalem. After a tentative economic recovery, stagnation dominated the latter half of the 1990s. Tourists came in waves, but like before, their visits to Bethlehem were often short-lived.

The new settlement of Har Homa was constructed in 1997, positioned directly opposite Bethlehem and neighboring Beit Sahour, during the tenure of Israeli Prime Minister Netanyahu's first government. Speculations circulated that Har Homa might emerge as a rival to Bethlehem, with the necessary tourist infrastructure possibly being developed for that purpose. It was even said that Bethlehem's holy sites might eventually transform into a museum lacking a living community.

The 1996 elections for the Palestinian Legislative Council initially appeared to signal a democratic start. However, skepticism lingered regarding the actual authority of the deputies, given the limited powers of the Palestinian Authority and the predominant role of President Yasser Arafat. I recall hearing people question the identities of those "photo models" featured on election posters.

Nevertheless, the time of Jara's birth in 1997 wasn't entirely devoid of hope. Personally, I enrolled in a guiding course at the Bethlehem Bible College, anticipating that Bethlehem 2000 could, if not a breakthrough, at least signify the commencement of an independent Palestinian tourism industry. Nonetheless, during Christmas in 1999 and the first half of 2000, the number of tourists who arrived fell below expectations.

The summer of that year witnessed the ill-fated Israeli-Palestinian-American Summit of Camp David in the United States. The brazen assertiveness of Israeli power clashed with the Palestinian Authority's inadequacies. On September 29, 2000, the second Intifada erupted following a provocative visit by then-Israeli opposition leader Sharon to the Muslim-controlled Haram al-Sharif in Jerusalem's Old City. The Intifada represented an eruption of pent-up anger. The Palestinian Authority, shaky and lacking direction, frequently tainted by corruption allegations, appeared to possess limited control over subsequent developments in Palestinian streets.

By the close of 2000, Bethlehem's identity was characterized not so much by the multifaceted cultural identity previously discussed, but rather by the painful identity of a victimized populace ensnared within a deeply oppressive and violent occupation system. Many young individuals joined the new Intifada, while a considerable majority observed from the sidelines. Bethlehem's identity was increasingly defined by the countless similar narratives exchanged daily among individuals in Bethlehem and across Palestine—stories of checkpoint humiliations and difficulties in securing travel permits. The construction of the Separation Wall, or as locals termed it, the Apartheid Wall, often extending deep into the West Bank, further entrenched the disparity between the occupier and the occupied.

Beyond serving as a source of inspiration, Bethlehem posed as a formidable challenge for foreigners like me. For several years, I worked as an education advisor, coinciding with the introduction of a new Palestinian curriculum in 2000. Young people and educators were in search of new, motivating activities that would offer them an active role and a future perspective within society. My interest encompassed education in its broadest

The Village, a City

sense—embracing learning processes, consciousness-raising, and access to educational resources beyond the classroom. The viewpoints of both youths and educators held significance for me. Education in Palestine unfolded amidst numerous diverse and educationally demanding experiences, which too often bred fleeting despair, yet also unearthed an hitherto untapped inner resilience within both educators and students.

From where did these wellsprings of strength emanate? In part, the answer lay in Palestinian sumud.[1] As an international who became increasingly immersed in Palestinian life, sumud to a certain extent molded my perception of Palestine and motivated me to pursue educational and consciousness-raising endeavors. Mary, through her way of life, epitomized and taught me the essence of this concept.

Literally translating to "steadfastness," the essence of sumud was discernible if not omnipresent among many Palestinians, regardless of whether they resided in rural areas, urban centers, refugee camps, or semi-desert regions. In its fundamental Palestinian interpretation, steadfastness symbolized the determination to remain on ancestral family lands, preserve an emotional bond with the Palestinian home, and uphold dignity while making the necessary compromises to ensure survival.

Historically, the understanding of sumud as the act of clinging to the land dates back to the early days of resistance against Zionist colonization in Palestine during the 1920s and 1930s, during the era of the British Mandate. It evolved into a prominent concept among Palestinians who remained under Israeli military rule in Israel after the Nakba [disaster] in 1948, the displacement or expulsion of over 700.000 Palestinians who fled the area which was to become Israel. Many of these individuals, often referred to as "48 Palestinians," drew cultural inspiration from the principle and practice of sumud. Literary figures like the poet and former mayor of Nazareth, Tawfiq Zayyad, likened the strength of Palestinian sumud to the deeply rooted olive tree. Sumud became a familiar notion among the hundreds of thousands of Palestinian refugees who resided outside their homeland after 1948, their sumud signifying the determination to maintain ties with the Palestinian land and uphold their national rights, including the right of return.

In the West Bank and Gaza during the 1970s, sumud transformed into a political rallying cry as local communities began to organize in opposition

---

1. For an overview of articles and interviews on sumud in the Bethlehem area, see Arab Educational Institute-Pax Christi, *Sumud Reader*.

The Birthplace of Jesus Is in Palestine

to the Israeli occupation since 1967. Sumud entreated Palestinians to remain steadfast, resist flight or migration from the land, and prevent another Nakba or *Naksa*—the latter referring to the "setback" of the 1967 war, during which hundreds of thousands of Palestinians once again crossed the Jordan River, often becoming refugees for a second time.

One early connotation of sumud in the occupied territories pertained to Palestinian demographics, the number of individuals residing on the land. Sumud even became associated with a high birth rate. By the late 1970s, the establishment of a Sumud Funds by the Palestinian Liberation Organization (PLO) in partnership with the Jordanian government and other Arab regimes aimed to economically support Palestinians in remaining on their land.

During the 1980s, Palestinian grassroots organizations like medical committees, agricultural committees, and women's committees proposed an alternative interpretation of sumud. Operating largely on volunteerism, these organizations endorsed a proactive development strategy, seeking to create conditions that would enable people to stay on the land and enhance the status of women, peasants, and health workers who confronted the mounting pressures of occupation on Palestinian society.

The years following the second Intifada in 2000 marked a renewed significance of the sumud concept. In the West Bank, Palestinians struggled to safeguard their livelihoods and dignity despite the mounting challenges of daily life within an increasingly confined living space. The Palestinian Authority, initially seen as a beacon of hope, gradually transformed into a symbol and embodiment of stagnation, corruption, and favoritism, exacerbated even more after the apparent assassination of the long-standing revolutionary figure Yasser Arafat in 2004. With traditional models of revolutionary struggle appearing less relevant and the established leadership becoming ensnared in patterns of dependency and cooptation by the occupying forces, people began searching for alternative sources of inspiration that embodied human dignity and resistance.

In parallel with the strategic and developmental application of sumud, there has always been a fascination among Palestinians with a more motivational and existential interpretation of the concept. At the heart of this perspective lies not only the practice of remaining on the land, as traditionally understood, or the strategies designed to empower communities and collectives to remain rooted, but also the inner resilience of individuals not to surrender, not to succumb to what might be perceived as psychological pitfalls, such as resignation, withdrawal, or a loss of self-control. This was especially relevant when the occupation seemed far from temporary and the political leadership struggled to command admiration.

This nuanced view is articulated in the early sumud diaries of Palestinian lawyer and author Raja Shehadeh[2], which marked the beginning of a series of documentary writings spanning multiple decades, exploring life under occupation beyond rhetoric. In Shehadeh's perspective, sumud represented a "third way" between succumbing to occupation on one hand and resorting to violence on the other. It entailed the steadfast pursuit of a dignified daily life despite immense pressures. This interpretation of sumud resonates with the "third way" philosophies within the broader global peace and nonviolence movements, where active resistance to oppressive systems serves as an alternative to submission and violent confrontation.

Amid the myriad examples of Palestinian sumud as an expression of moral agency, there are well-known stories of resolute defense—the family persistently inhabiting their ancestral home despite the nearby presence of settlements, walls, or checkpoints; the individual standing in the path of a bulldozer and refusing to yield; or the family rebuilding their "illegal" home after multiple demolitions.

However, while these archetypal manifestations of sumud are familiar to Palestinians and their supporters, its most remarkable aspect within this broader existential framework is its adaptability across countless forms. With all its demands—and for some, sumud might be more of an ideal than a daily reality—it is a democratic concept that accommodates a diversity of participation. The experiences that test people's resolve and their moral responses are comparable yet distinct. This democratic and inclusive dimension renders sumud relevant to the realm of education as well.

Through its focus on strength and dealing with obstacles the concept of sumud lends itself very well to stories. While staying in Bethlehem, I consistently approached education through the methods of story-writing and story-telling. This interest originated during my PhD research in Holland, where I researched Western popular literature and its narrative stereotypes of Palestine and Israel.

Since the inception of the second Intifada or uprising in the West Bank and Gaza in October 2000, I have been maintaining notes and writing blogs to comprehend an increasingly unjust and violent environment while also keeping friends and family abroad informed. Striving to integrate the

---

2. Shehadeh, *Third Way*.

viewpoints of an insider familiar with Palestinian life and an outsider-foreigner who maintains a degree of detachment, I chronicled diary entries to recount those valuable instances when Palestinians exhibit human dignity and agency while confronting adversity, oppression, and humiliation. As an anthropologist by training, I am intrigued by observing and narrating forms of everyday moral agency. It is this curiosity that underpins the dual purpose of this present book: offering a personal and familial portrayal of Palestinian day-to-day existence under occupation while also delving into the exploration of what it means to persist in the moral battle for human dignity—or in essence, what it signifies to remain steadfast, to keep one's sumud.

A CHRISTMAS LETTER TO MY UNBORN CHILD

Some time ago, your mother, carrying you in her belly, had a fantasy. She thought it would be nice if there was a little panel she could open to briefly look at you, to see if everything was fine, and to wonder about the color of your hair. Then she would be satisfied and keep the door locked until you were born.

Now, my wish is to send a little Christmas card through that opening. Why? Like your mom, to say hi and to tell you that you will enter the world in an uncommon place —Bethlehem—a small town with a famous past and a complicated present. A town conducive to dreams and wishes, but also a town reaching towards the year 2000 in a yet unborn country undergoing difficult labors.

What are my Christmas wishes? Don't worry; I don't have big wishes. I don't wish you to be a boy or a girl. I don't wish you to be Dutch or Palestinian. I don't wish you to stay in Bethlehem or live elsewhere. Nor do I mind whether you will love books, music, or beautiful designs. Your mother and I hope to follow Khalil Jibran, who advises parents to give their children love but not their thoughts.

But I do have a few small wishes. I hope you will hear many fairy tales and not just stories from reality. I wish that you will laugh and experience the warmth of Palestinian culture, as well as the sobriety of Dutch culture.

I wish that you will not be bothered by traffic, soldiers, and noise. I wish that you will have the chance to see the beauty of nature rather than the ugliness of waste. I wish that you will not be confined by closures and that you can go in all directions to see Palestine, Holland, and the world.

The Village, a City

I hope to see and hear you soon.

Your father
December 19, 1997

Jara [pronounced as Yara] was born on December 21, 1997, at the Holy Family Hospital in Bethlehem.

FIGURE 1

Church of the Nativity

2

Housebound

THROUGHOUT THE SECOND INTIFADA, spanning roughly from 2000 to 2004, the Israeli occupation penetrated the most intimate spaces: our homes and the immediate surroundings, including the gardens adjacent to my mother-in-law's house where our family sought refuge during Easter 2002 and its aftermath. Israeli army-imposed curfews lasted for weeks on end, confining us around the clock, with limited breaks for essential purchases allowed only every few days. The initial curfew of five weeks materialized following a situation in which around 200 militants took refuge in the Church of the Nativity, under the protection of priests. Subsequently, a large-scale Israeli military operation unfolded, with tanks, soldiers, and military equipment entering Bethlehem's heart. Thankfully, Mary had just given birth to our second child, Tamer, in a nearby hospital and managed to return home before the curfew's imposition.

Daily life was wrested from our grasp. The length of each curfew remained uncertain, as did the factors that influenced its extension or removal. Questions hung heavily: What about school for the children, including Jara? How would it affect our work, studies, and movement? The sense of agency evaporated, our physical and mental spaces contracting. How could we shield our minds from the onslaught of worry and anxiety? To what extent did our thoughts become dominated by the constant sight of obstacles? How much room could our children find to play in the immediate vicinity, be it the house, the garden, or its boundaries? How much room remained for simply living, for the essence of human existence?

In this context, sumud morphed into a refusal to be paralyzed by the circumstances, a commitment to uphold the rituals of daily family life adapted to the dire conditions.

⌁

4 April 2002: Early in the morning, the third day of the occupation. Should I even utter "good morning" to the family? I take a short walk of about fifteen meters to glance through a gate. The tank on the university hill maintains its position. On a nearby doctor's rooftop, Israeli sharpshooters are stationed. I retreat swiftly. Just yesterday, Jara, who is four years old, cautioned that the tank would shoot me if I dared to take out the garbage bags. We're effectively trapped. Nobody leaves their homes. This is a closed military zone. Every so often, one or more tanks rumble by, their noise intimidating, some even flaunting Israeli flags. As if there could be any room for misunderstanding. Only once do we catch the distant wail of an ambulance, an exception that's allowed passage.

We're here, six of us, at my in-laws'. Mary, Jara, our newborn son Tamer, Mary's sister Janet, my mother-in-law, and myself. Fortuitously, Tamer—his name means "holder of dates" symbolizing abundance of life—was born just days before the occupation began. Presently, no medical assistance can reach Bethlehem's homes. Mary managed to return home after giving birth. However, our hearts ache even more than usual upon learning of a baby who perished during childbirth because, due to the soldiers entering the city, the mother couldn't access the hospital on time.

We made the decision to seek refuge at my in-laws' home, primarily to provide each other with better support but also due to our own home's proximity to the 'Azza refugee camp which could potentially become a target for searches by soldiers.

⌁

The initial day of the occupation, Tuesday, unfolded without electricity. In the evening, we lit candles and retired to bed early. In the darkness, I recounted children's stories to Jara—tales of jungles and perilous animals. Playacting as Tarzan, she leapt from the bed into my awaiting arms, my limbs outstretched like branches. I'm taken aback by how well she's handling the situation. She crafts drawings that resemble images from a dream

The Birthplace of Jesus Is in Palestine

world: idyllic peaceful houses populated by birds and dancing children. She's fairly aware of the events underway and has her own playful nicknames for Israeli Prime Minister Sharon. Yet, she hasn't quite grasped how extraordinary our current circumstances are. "We have many tanks here, do you have them too?" she lightly inquires of Mary's sister, who's calling from Paris. While I tenderly croon love songs to Tamer—the world's most beautiful baby—Jara interrupts the ambiance, gesturing towards the window and asking, "Is that the sound of a tank?"

At the moment, we're managing with our supplies. Unlike other parts of Bethlehem, we're fortunate to have electricity, water, and an adequate food supply, and the telephone line is functional. There was a surge in shopping at supermarkets and vegetable markets before the invasion, and there has been a recent scarcity of fresh fruits and vegetables. We have enough food to last us at least a week. However, different areas of Bethlehem are grappling with lack of phone and/or electricity service. In 'Azza, 'Aida, and Dheisheh refugee camps, there is neither water nor electricity. We're informed via the Internet that the water supply for over hundred thousand people has been momentarily cut off in Ramallah. Will that fate befall us too? No one knows. At least we've managed to stockpile enough bottled water for the baby. There's also a sufficient amount of paper for Jara's drawings. I've decided to let my beard grow for the duration of the occupation. How long will it become?

At least we have enough space, and I've designated a corner in the bedroom of my in-laws' house for the computer, which will be transferred from our own home.

Numerous members of Mary's family are involved in municipal activities. The city hall is now under Israeli control, and the staff is confined to one room. A cousin is spearheading relief efforts at the Church of the Nativity, where many are trapped. It remains uncertain whether they are armed, though church authorities deny it. They're in dire need of food, which is in short supply. Multiple wounded individuals lack medical care. It's safe to assume that numerous people in Bethlehem are facing a shortage of proper medical treatment. Tanks ran over two parked ambulance cars in Wadi Ma'aleh, not far from the Church of the Nativity. Additionally, the Orthodox clinic in Beit Sahour, an important local medical facility, was invaded. A wounded patient was arrested and taken away, and local television reports state that medical equipment was damaged or destroyed during the incursion. One particularly tragic circumstance is the prohibition against burying the deceased. While we lack precise figures for the number of fatalities over the past two days, the toll likely stands close to ten.

One idea we're considering at work is to urge local teachers who have email access at home to write diaries, collate them, and send them abroad. Similar initiatives have been undertaken in Ramallah. Despite being confined, we can at least attempt to cultivate a collective voice amid a world that appears shockingly paralyzed.

Back at home, Mary requests that I retrieve a digital camera from our friend and neighbor, who is not far from us but has temporarily gone to Jerusalem. We want to capture photos of our newborn baby, Tamer, and send them to family abroad, as well as to relatives and friends in Bethlehem. Jara insists on joining us. Mary explains that after Jara saw Janet and me leave, she found the courage and now wants to venture outside too. I have reservations, but Mary gives her approval. While we watch the tanks stationed at the university, Jara holds my hand with a tight grip. She marches on and receives sweets from someone who spots us entering our friend's house.

Upon returning home, I realize that we lack the needed computer disk for the camera. We have just half an hour before being confined once again, so I hurry down the university road to our own house, located opposite the ʻAzza refugee camp. Suddenly, gunfire erupts, and I see kids from the camp running toward their homes. They likely provoked a tank or a patrol. In the days prior to the invasion, I witnessed them playing *shaheed* [martyr]; they chanted slogans and carried a makeshift coffin over their heads, symbolizing a burial. I'm uncertain whether to continue on my way. The inhabitants of a nearby house wave me to come inside. Some of them suggest I take a route through the gardens and climb over a wall. After the gunfire ceases, I return to the main road and reach my house. The phone is ringing. It's Mary. She briefly believed that I had been shot and asks me to take a different route back.

Outside, I water the plants. The neighbors sit peacefully in their garden, enjoying the wonderful weather. They inquire if it's wise for us to be outside our house, given the risk that soldiers might blow up the door. I return home, and Mary tells me that she had a glass of *ʻarak*, an anise-flavored alcoholic drink, to calm her nerves after our conversation. She was genuinely frightened; the gunfire sounded so close, and I was the only person on the street.

The following day, Saturday, we hear from friends in Beit Jala that local soldier patrols announced the curfew in the evening while taunting the population: "Dear people of Beit Jala, you are good people, have sweet dreams." During the day, I play with Jara in the garden, but I feel restless. I don't want her to pick up on my nervousness. Jara is in a rebellious mood, suggesting she wants to put wet grass on the street to make the tanks slip. She plays the role of a sleeping princess, waiting for a kiss from a prince to awaken her. However, when I kiss her, she claims that she has already died.

Janet and I retrieve the laundry, but when heavy gunfire suddenly erupts nearby, Jara, Janet, and I quickly rush back inside the house. Now Jara realizes that this isn't a game. The days when we could attribute shootings and bombardments to St George—a local patron saint—splitting the skies are gone. The latest news, as Mary shares, is that many people have been killed in Jenin in the northern West Bank. The Church of the Nativity is still under siege. Amidst all this, a desperate question forms in my mind; a question that seems out of place: How can we find a way to engage in dialogue with the Israelis after all that has transpired?

6 April: I spot Fuad, the Institute's director, speaking to an interviewer, explaining how every house on central Madbasseh street has been hit by bullets or worse. We hurry into a pharmacy, our primary destination, armed with a long list of medications that Mary and her mother require. The pharmacist's wife dashes around the shop, serving customers quickly, reminiscent of the service at a busy Dutch fried potato stand during peak season. Time is uncertain, and shopkeepers aim to assist everyone efficiently. There's a long line outside the supermarket as well. With bread unavailable, Janet inquires across the queue about the availability of flour; and indeed, they have some.

8 April: A social worker friend of ours is constantly receiving calls from people in the area seeking advice: What should they do with their children? How can they find food? She learned that across from the mosque at Manger Square, soldiers have occupied the second floor of a family's house. They've vandalized the rooms, destroyed furniture, and even left excrement on the floor. Other families in the old downtown part of Bethlehem have been driven away or forced to take refuge in specific sections of their homes, particularly in buildings chosen by sharpshooters.

On local TV, we see an Israeli balloon hovering over the Church of the Nativity complex. It appears to be equipped with cameras, potentially recording events in and around the area. The goal might be to identify any attempts to deliver food to the church, where both the clergy and the *Tanzim*, a Palestinian armed group, are facing severe shortages.

In our area, we manage. Unlike others, we have access to electricity, water, and telephone service. We can also leave the house for a short time every three days. It's possible that shops may run out of supplies eventually, but our situation pales in comparison to what's happening in a city like Jenin. Mary recounts how she heard a mother on the radio describing how bulldozers razed her house to make room for a road through the camp. During the interview, the mother was frantically searching for her three-year-old child who might be trapped under the rubble.

We think of Jara, and we don't think. As we fill Tamer's bathtub, we prepare ourselves for one of those small rituals of daily life that we cannot help but cherish. Through Tamer, it feels as if we're holding on to life.

It's inevitable that children would yearn to go outside after being confined for a week, especially with the delightful spring weather. Birds sing inviting songs, and some gardens are explored hesitantly. Jara has connected with the neighbors' children and wants to play with them. I assist her in climbing over the rocks into the neighbor's courtyard. The usual street entrance is off-limits. During the curfew, nobody dares to venture onto the streets, except for a lone journalist who somehow managed to enter our area in Bethlehem. He walks with his hands raised, holding a white flag in one hand.

Some of Jara's play reflects the political situation. Yesterday, she asked me to stretch out my hands as if to handcuff me and put me in prison. In reality, there are hundreds of blindfolded and handcuffed men from the Bethlehem area who are currently held in a military camp atop Beit Jala. In another game, Jara takes a tree branch and pretends it's a walking stick, acting as a man injured by Israeli gunfire. Then, she picks up the branch and mimics the action of shooting. Like any child, she brags in front of the other kids that she's part of the *shabab*, the young men engaged in resistance. She parades with her chest out, shouting, "*as-sha'ab al-'arabi ween*"—where are the Arab people?—a familiar song frequently played on local TV. Amid her laughter, she reassures the other kids not to be afraid. She simplifies the world into people who shoot and people who don't. When we see Tony Blair on TV, she suddenly asks, "Does he shoot?" And even as we dream of swimming once this ordeal is over, she refuses to go to a swimming pool in Jerusalem, fearing, "the Israelis will shoot us there."

Though I usually find the persistent car honking irritating, I now yearn for something other than the eerie quiet hanging over Bethlehem. Yesterday morning, a prolonged siren sounded. I hurried outside, thinking there might be an emergency, only to realize it was a siren commemorating the Holocaust victims. Due to the proximity of the Gilo settlement, we hear the siren nearly as loudly as in any part of Israel.

More vibrant sounds emerge. Jara and I play with the neighbor's dog in their garden. The dog barks at another dog, which replies, a cat joins in, Jara's friend imitates monkey sounds, and suddenly, a jungle springs to life. Neighbors peek out of their windows. A semblance of normalcy. Then, a distant gunshot breaks the air. Silence swiftly follows, and even as time passes, the voices of life return hesitantly, never quite at ease.

Nighttime silence can be ominous too. When the neighbor's dog barks at night, we worry that soldiers are nearby. The dog doesn't bark without reason. Both during the day and night, we hear sporadic gunfire, a single shot or the rapid burst of heavy gunfire. We can't ascertain its source or target.

Walking the streets during curfew is undeniably perilous. Last Tuesday, a desperate man from Bethlehem ventured to Beit Jala during the limited opening hours there to find food. He was shot and killed at the Baab al-Zqaaq junction, a mere two hundred meters from our home. On Friday, a man in Beit Sahour was fatally shot in a hail of bullets while trying to open his shop for the soldiers to prevent them from blowing up his door. I hear stories of people hiding under their beds for prolonged periods during gunfire, helicopter flights, or tank movements. "They shoot at every *dubbaaneh* [fly]," Janet remarks.

The exhaustion, despondency, and nervousness among the people are growing. It's not just the feeling of being immobilized but also the relentless assault—under the pretext of defense—on Palestinian society as a whole. The influx of distressing news reaches a point where one feels utterly powerless. We're taken aback to learn that Mary's uncle's lands are now being leveled for a road leading to Har Homa, the settlement north of Bethlehem. As if the present occupation wasn't enough. The cumulative weight of distressing news, concern for loved ones, worry about property, and the sound of gunfire outside are all fraying our nerves.

However, our home remains a space that hasn't been invaded yet. We keep it impeccably clean. We've consumed all the Easter cookies, originally intended for visitors, ourselves. Of course, the children largely dictate the rhythm of life; the regular milk feeds, baths, the food that Jara doesn't want to eat. The children keep us occupied. In the evenings, I don't attempt to watch movies. Any form of escapism is jolted back to reality, like a cold shower.

Thankfully, Jara can venture outside within our neighborhood to interact with neighbors' children, climbing through the gardens. Yesterday, when we heard the sound of approaching tanks and gunfire, Jara quickly clung to my legs. Within a minute, she resumed playing. When we called her back home, she began to argue: "Mama, the tank is near Gaby [five hundred meters away, which means it's far enough]. Don't be afraid." She learns from the neighbors' kids that placing grass on the streets won't deter the tanks; rocks are needed. Her main interest lies in playing with the ball. When the ball falls into another neighbor's garden, I rush to retrieve it and throw it back, but Jara can't be pacified. I should have brought her to the ball so she could throw it back herself.

For Tamer, I sing old songs by Mama Cass, "There Is a New World Coming" and "Dream a Little Dream of Me." As tanks and armored personnel carriers pass by, I raise my voice. Tamer continues to sleep peacefully, occasionally opening his eyes to gaze into the sunlight.

---

14 February: The most significant occurrences in our confined world are the announcements of temporary curfew lifts. On Friday afternoon, Mary compiles a list of necessities to buy. We divide the tasks since we have only a few hours outside, and neighbors might drop by for visits. After two weeks of curfew, there's no more milk, fresh fruits, vegetables, or *tahini* (a sesame seed sauce used to make *dibis*, a popular grape syrup spread here). Janet and I exchange quick conversations on the street: "How are you? (*bitjannen* – terrific). Do you have water, telephone, electricity? No house searches?"

The Birthplace of Jesus Is in Palestine

People rush off to complete their tasks. At Kattan's shop on Manger Road, the shopkeeper is out of regular plastic bags, so he packs my purchases in eight small Gauloises cigarette bags. Luckily, pharmacies still sell diapers and baby formula. The Hazboun supermarket on Madbasseh Street is so crowded that Jara gets anxious.

22 April: Over three weeks of curfew make time lose its significance once more. The calls to prayer from the mosques and the ringing of church bells are absent, except for the "opening hours" when we are allowed to step outside. My neighbor and I have a playful competition to see who can grow the longest beard by the end of the Bethlehem occupation. Last week, when daylight saving time was introduced in the West Bank, Mary and her family decided that it doesn't matter much, with no work or school; it's better to stick with the old time, as if staying detached from the flow of time. In fact, Mary and I sometimes forget which day of the week it is.

While the curfew's opening hours mark significant moments, they're ambiguous; sometimes dreadful, sometimes pleasant. You need to accomplish a lot in that brief window, including shopping (long queues, especially for coveted items like tomatoes—you have to rush out as soon as the hour begins), taking Tamer to the doctor for vaccinations, and, on the bright side, welcoming visitors and family who want to congratulate us and meet Tamer for the first time. An overpowering stench emanates from garbage piles at every street corner, the sand on the streets leaves you yearning for a bath afterward, the fallen streetlights and electric poles, and of course, the tanks that brazenly fire into the air merely for intimidation.

On Sunday, a new development unfolds. Mary casually says, "They're going from house to house." I inquire, "Who, the people from the food convoy or the march?" Both a food convoy and religious marchers were supposed to enter Bethlehem that day. Mary clarifies, "No, the soldiers." A neighbor across the street calls to inform us that soldiers entered her house twice—once during the day and once in the evening. Her family was told to stay outside while the soldiers conducted a search. Afterward, the soldiers left tools to break the door of their upstairs neighbor. We also hear that soldiers attempted to enter our house, damaging the door in the process, but they didn't succeed.

Mary looks outside and witnesses around twenty soldiers entering houses. Some go indoors while others stand guard. People peek through windows. Jara joins the window watching and spots a soldier urinating near a gate that leads to our house. "He shouldn't pee on the ground, that's dirty," she comments. She starts chanting her verse: "*batteech, shamaam, sharon zaghlek fil hammaam*" [watermelon, yellow melon, Sharon slips in the toilet]. She asks me to follow her; we are playing the Israeli army. She grabs a plastic knife as her gun and starts shouting "*shalom aleichem*." After a while, we glance through the door window to see that our own house, about two hundred meters downhill, is encircled by soldiers. Mary feels concerned, and I try to console her. "At least we took out all the valuables," I say. She responds, "It's not about the valuables, it's the principle." The soldiers come and go; we can't see if they've entered as our door is out of sight. Later, neighbors inform us that windows were broken but the soldiers didn't enter. So we were fortunate. However, our neighbor next door, Emile Jarjou'eh, wasn't as lucky. He's the head of a ministerial committee for Muslim-Christian relations in the Palestinian National Authority. His house underwent intense shooting; apparently, the soldiers forced their way in. Could they have thought our house was linked to the PNA?

Jara wonders if the soldiers shoot at birds. Recently, while playing in the garden, she has developed an affection for birds. Neighbors are calling each other, but the lines are busy. "Have they entered?" "Not yet." One neighbor prays incessantly. I assure Jara that there's no need to be afraid. "Papa is a foreigner, and they won't harm foreigners and their families." I tell her that even if the soldiers enter, we can still share our story with journalists and others. We can always do something, that's the message I convey to her. What else can you say?

Then the soldiers approach our house. Jara panics and hides under a pillow. Mary opens the door, and there are five soldiers. They want to see the men's IDs. Mary explains that there are two men in the house: myself, a Dutchman, and a three-week-old baby. Somewhat childishly, I relish standing on the doorstep, trying to appear taller than the soldiers. I show them my passport. The five men seem bashful. Only the commander inspects more closely; checking cupboards, under mattresses, and beneath beds. "Do you think there are people hiding there?" Mary asks. "We're searching for weapons," they reply. Initially, Mary wants to prevent them from entering the baby's room, but I allow the commander, provided he remains silent. Luckily, he's respectful.

The Birthplace of Jesus Is in Palestine

Jara is calmer now. After the soldiers leave, she wants to play outside. I think it's best for her to release her tension, so we play in the garden, with a group of soldiers initially allowing it. However, they eventually ask us to return indoors. We go inside for a bit and then venture outside again to play with the neighbor's dog—all under the soldiers' watchful eyes. I decide to remain outside, hoping to make them aware of a foreign presence, whatever difference that might make. At one point, the soldiers say in English, "Behave yourself," directed at the barking dog.

They inquire if we have the neighbors' key. Mary knows they are likely upstairs, possibly hiding. She asks the soldiers if they rather want to search the nearby house of a good friend who is not present. She wants to avoid the soldiers breaking the door. I guide a soldier to the location, but they decline to enter. "Who knows why," Mary responds.

Some soldiers sit on the ground, appearing bored. Mary initiates an argument, upset about the damage to our house. The soldiers respond, "We're looking for Hamas." "Who created Hamas?" Mary retorts. "Sharon is a bigger terrorist than Hamas." A soldier comments, "We gave you 96%." "We want 100%," Mary says indignantly. When asked about Arafat's corruption, she counters, "That's our problem. Why are you breaking the glass of our home?" The commander initially denies anything being broken, but then acknowledges it with a shrug. When Mary questions him about Jenin, he remains silent. "He couldn't say anything," Mary concludes. My own interactions with the soldiers are less confrontational, but I refrain from greeting or offering niceties when they begin to praise Jara's appearance.

Jara shares with the neighbor's son what happened, explaining, "Papa opened the cupboards, they looked, and *khalas* [that was it]." The neighbor expresses concern as the soldiers took their IDs and Latin American passports. Phone calls continue. Someone in the neighborhood reports that the soldiers took his binoculars. A friend of Mary's calls, worried they might take her son. In the meantime, a few houses down, soldiers have occupied the house of an absent lawyer for sleeping, eating, and whatever else they do.

❦

The following day, during the opening hours, we visit our house. The locker and door are severely damaged, with boot marks visible. We can't enter through the main door; they had apparently attempted to force their way in with basic tools. A curtain was pulled down through a window, and several windowpanes are shattered. We manage to enter through a side door, remove the broken glass, and cover the openings. Then we go to our neighbor Emile Jarjou'eh's house, which is in disarray: broken computers, printers, files strewn on the floor, a large photo of Arafat shot to pieces, even an image of the Last Supper defaced. Outside, two cars have been shot through. We take photos. Mary and I discuss how soldiers who seem polite can unleash themselves when foreigners aren't watching. It's a double face.

On May 3rd, Jara and I play in the neighbor's garden under the pleasant Mediterranean sun. She asks the neighbor, "Do you have everything?" This has become a routine question as people show concern for each other. A tank's rolling sound is audible in the distance, resembling a massive washing machine. Jara dashes to a corner of the garden to get a glimpse. She's learned from other kids about different types of tanks, like the *dabaabeh* and the *mujanzareh*. Mary and I don't even know the differences.

Jara wants to play. We imagine the school at one corner of the garden, our house at the opposite corner, and the shops at another end. As if we're kids of the same age, we have breakfast and then Jara pretends to go to school. She runs and shouts, "Quick, quick, the soldiers are doing pow-pow," pointing at me as if protecting her little friend. While running, she screams with joyful fear, much like when she plays with the dog. After our counting exercises at "school," Jara opens the imaginary door of the garden house, puts her hand over her mouth, and pretends to be shocked. "Look! Everything is broken. The bedroom, the dining room, even the kitchen." She likely recalls the images of the damaged house of Jarjou'eh that we visited a few days earlier. I ask her to tell the journalists what happened. "Yes, yes, all the journalists should know," she agrees. Then we play at shopping, pretending to buy a new TV and couches from the "shopping section" of the garden. At least she's learning that she can take action to change a situation. Helplessness is the worst feeling, and I hope we can avoid it.

Jara recounts that she dreamt of being a good witch confronted by a bad one who wanted to enter her house. She, Papa, and her little brother refused entry to the bad witch, and she jumped into the air, shooting the intruder dead. Currently, she's captivated by fairy tales where a wolf or fox threatens a home. While I can't shake my inherent sober convictions, which seem to lose relevance daily, I'm pleased that her stories offer peaceful solutions: the fox is scared away, the wolf is safely taken to a distant forest.

The Birthplace of Jesus Is in Palestine

On May 11, the long siege of the Church of the Nativity and the curfew in Bethlehem finally come to an end after almost six weeks. Mary and Janet are glued to Al Jazeera for updates, as this satellite station is a major source of news for the Bethlehemites. Guevara al-Budeiri, a correspondent, reports with intensity and emotion, emphasizing that Bethlehem is occupied. She and her colleague in Ramallah, Shireen Abu Akleh, become role models for the youth in the area. Jara even spots Tony Salman, Mary's cousin, on TV; he had been in the church serving as a liaison between the priests and militants.

However, the resolution feels somewhat anticlimactic for many Bethlehemites. While relieved to leave their houses, there's sadness and mixed feelings about the compromise reached. The situation raises questions about the Palestinian right of return conflicting with the agreement involving deportation. Mary and others feel a combination of relief and sadness. The militants emerging from the church and waving to their family members they can't say goodbye to brings tears to Mary's eyes. A group arriving in Gaza is interviewed by Palestine TV, and their loved ones call them in the studio, knowing they may not meet again for years. One of them mentions seeing the sea for the first time. Many young people in the West Bank have never had the chance to leave the area.

Mary plays with Tamer on her lap, gently tickling his chin to elicit a laugh. Soon, like other new parents in the area, we plan to visit the Church of the Nativity. We intend to lay Tamer on the Star, a symbol of Jesus's birthplace, which had also served as a refuge for militants for a period. We hope to capture a photograph of him there, creating an icon that represents a brighter future.

On June 21, Mary and I stroll slowly together along the narrow path in front of our family house. We're supporting her elderly mother, who's over ninety years old. The *askedinyeh* [loquat] tree in the garden is adorned with its vibrant orange fruits. Mary points out the barely visible clusters of grapes, explaining that it's the ideal time to collect grape leaves. These sour leaves are often used in Arab meals to wrap bundles of rice and meat. She also gestures to the spot where the family dog, Lubo, was once laid to rest. At the end of the road lies a small children's graveyard, earning the street

Housebound

the nickname "Children's Street." I recall a playful incident on April 1 when I pranked Mary with a fake snake.

Later, I leisurely stroll with Jara along the university street. Typically bustling with students carrying books to the nearby university, the street now lies devoid of cars. A calm ambiance prevails, marked by the gentle whistling of birds and intermittent bursts of sunlight through the clouds. Jara spots playful shapes in the clouds, imagining a crocodile among them. A neighbor introduces us to their adorable puppy. Our interactions with neighbors are frequent, revealing the unique bonds formed during these days. It's reminiscent of the leisurely afternoons in traditional Palestinian villages when people find solace in simple activities in front of the home.

Though the curfew is less stringent this time, it remains an annoyance. Children are venturing further outside, their voices echoing through the streets, but they quickly retreat to gardens upon hearing the telltale sounds of approaching tanks or armored personnel carriers (APCs). Once the tanks recede, their playful voices reemerge. Some children even mimic the eerie wails of military sirens and the broadcasts announcing curfew with remarkable accuracy.

Parents may think that soldiers won't arrest their young children, or perhaps they find it difficult to control them. I recall an incident with Brahim, a neighbor, who playfully teased Jara by telling her not to go outside. In response, she pointed her finger in the distance and confidently remarked, "*shu ya'ani* [What's the matter], the *mamnu'a el-tajawoul* [curfew, lit. forbidden to go around] is not for here but for there." Occasionally, we hear variations in the otherwise monotonous and thoughtless *mamnu'a* phrase. In Beit Jala, the jeeps have even reversed the words violating the grammatical rules, repeating "*mamnu'a el-tajawoul, el-tajawoul mamnu'a.*" They go a step further by taunting people with the question, "Where are the millions?"—a reference to a verse from the song "*ween al 'arabi?*" [where are the Arabs?], a tune that Jara enjoys singing.

※

July 6: the word "crocodile" might not be the best way to describe the imposing machine that prowls our streets. It resembles more of a dragon, both in appearance and sound. During late afternoons, when the weather cools down slightly, the University Road becomes alive with numerous children. To an observer, it might seem like a charming scene. The sight of kids playing on an empty street brings to mind the memory of the "*autoloze zondag*" [car-free Sunday] that was temporarily introduced in the Netherlands in 1973 due to oil shortages. On those Sundays, highways were taken over by cyclists reveling in the freedom of the carless roads. Some neighbors lean against the sidewalls, relaxed, while kids play games. About a week ago, Janet gave Jara a scooter, and she now proudly showcases it to the other children in the street. With a growing volume in her voice, she calls out to her friends: "Marwan, Marwaaaan, 'Diiiiima," trying to capture everyone's attention. Last week, she was hardly home as she moved from neighbor to neighbor. However, by evening, she was unwell and ended up vomiting. Perhaps an excess of sweets was the cause?

At one point, the dragon-like machine observed the children playing and seemed displeased. With its deafening screech, it climbed towards the top of the university hill, releasing a loud noise as a warning to families. To ensure its intentions were understood, it returned several times to clear the street. Like the tides, the children retreated—sometimes behind a gate, or further into a garden, and as a final refuge, into their homes. However, they always returned once the monstrous presence disappeared from sight. One wise child, beyond his years, told Mary, "We've grown used to living with the *dabaabeh* [tank]."

The following day, Mary witnessed the tank stopping in the middle of the road. It turned off its engine, rotated its barrel, and emitted a strong smell of gasoline and dust. Mary had to close the windows to keep the smell out. I imagined a furious beast from movies, its neck swaying as it exhaled fire and smoke, leaving marks on the ground. The mayor of Bethlehem recently mentioned that according to Israeli law, tanks aren't allowed on Israeli streets due to the damage they cause. However, the streets of Bethlehem, much like the main roads in the West Bank, now bear the furrows left behind by these beasts.

Subsequently, Mary cautioned me against using my usual route through the gardens to reach our house, fearing it might arouse suspicion among the soldiers. Now, I occasionally venture out in the afternoon only after carefully listening for children's voices around to ensure the tanks are absent. Another reassuring signal is the sight of women on the high rooftops of nearby 'Azza camp, hanging freshly laundered linen on the lines while keeping a watchful eye on the streets below.

On another evening, I hear two loud bangs. Upon returning to Mary's, she informs me that soldiers had noticed our neighbor standing in the street, prompting them to fire a warning shot in our direction. The shot hit low on the electricity pole in front of our gate. Mary shows me the hole, which incidentally is the spot where Jara and the other kids usually play.

※

January 1, 2003, is the date for a significant celebration. At least, that's our intention. We have planned Tamer's baptism for this day, a festivity that is extensively observed in this region, often accompanied by a reception. We chose January 1, believing it would be free from curfew restrictions. However, early in the morning, it seems there is curfew in effect. To Mary's relief, though, the TV announces the lifting of the curfew. Oddly, two tanks patrol the main streets of Bethlehem, announcing the curfew. This leaves us confused about what's happening.

Mary makes phone calls, but nobody, not even the governor, comprehends the situation. Local TV states that the Israeli army headquarters reaffirms the curfew lift, yet outside, the tanks continue to chase cars and people off the streets. Speculation arises that the tanks might be acting without proper authorization, possibly to unnerve the people. Over the phone, Mary is in tears. First, she informs the restaurant that the reception for 90 people is canceled, then reconfirms it, and now she's uncertain. Finally, with a burst of determination and some sound advice, she declares, "*khalas* [enough], if the Israelis don't know what they're doing, we should know what we're doing, curfew or not." So we proceed.

The restaurant owner cooperates but requires an additional hour to prepare the food. We postpone the baptism by an hour. The bakery contacts us about the cake; due to the presence of the tanks, they are hesitant to deliver it to the restaurant. I take a taxi to the bakery, where the baker hastily adds "Tamer's baptism 1/1/2003" to the cake. Walking to the restaurant across from the Church of the Nativity, I notice a tank following me at a slow pace. The restaurant owner invites me inside, sighing with resignation, "See how we live."

The baptism turns out to be the festive occasion we had hoped for. During the ceremony, there's a flurry of video and photo cameras, making Tamer appear almost like a media sensation. When he lets out a small burble, Father Peter from Bethlehem University, who is conducting the baptism, remarks that he is "full of holiness," prompting laughter from all of us. As Father Peter later notes, the baptism was an event rather than a routine procedure. Families and friends enjoy the reception. As a colleague of Mary puts it, "anything uplifting is good for us." We capture a group photo of the Salman and Morcos families, their faces lit with joyful smiles, as if living in more favorable times. Some family and friends advise Mary against allowing people to kiss Tamer, fearing the evil eye, especially given his undeniable charm that might trigger a hint of jealousy (which, according to tradition, can attract the evil eye's attention).

⌇

As parents, it held great significance for us to uphold the small rituals associated with the needs of both Jara and Tamer, encompassing both necessities and moments of joy. These routines served as a lifeline, offering a sense of achievement even in the face of our challenging circumstances. Maintaining these daily rhythms and rituals provided a feeling of achieving "small victories" in the realm of human existence.

In this context, it's important to recognize that educating children is not a one-sided process. Children, in turn, impart wisdom and vitality to parents, particularly in a situation that could easily lead to paralysis. Children possess an innate drive to move forward, to avoid stagnation, and to resist being confined. Despite the challenging conditions, there were many instances where we found ourselves laughing alongside them or deriving humor from the circumstances. Through their games, dreams, and make-believe tales, children offer valuable lessons to adults. Their presence emitted love and lightheartedness, standing as a living testament against the senselessness of war and oppression. Reflecting on it now, I'm amazed at how the simple acts of playing, rhyming, and joking contributed to our inner resilience. These activities served as our form of anti-trauma therapy, helping us manage our emotions and stress.

Of course, not all games were light-hearted. Jara would pretend to "shoot" at people around her, and we observed children reenacting martyr's funerals. It was our role as adults and parents to ensure that the gravity of the situation didn't overpower and dominate the games and plays of the children and ourselves. This was essential to prevent a collective descent into depression and a loss of moral agency. People craved the occasional lighthearted remarks made by others on the street and within our community about "the Situation." In a way, these playful interactions highlighted the absurdity of it all, offering a moment of respite and perspective.

A few years later, Adnan Musallem, a history lecturer at Bethlehem University, provided an insightful explanation of sumud. He defined sumud as a "broad, active, and human concept" that revolves around not allowing oneself to be dehumanized. He gave an example to illustrate this point. According to him, part of asserting your presence in Palestine involves retaining your ability to laugh. Laughter serves as a defense mechanism. "When you laugh, chat, and joke, it enables you to continue being a human being. When you become entirely pessimistic, you're essentially saying, 'I'm ready to die, I don't want to live anymore.' This leads to self-dehumanization. Humor becomes essential in order to stand up and remain steadfast. It's a way of saying, 'I'm here, and no one can deny my presence here.'"[1]

In essence, he conveyed how humor is an integral part of upholding one's humanity in the face of adversity. It allows individuals to maintain their strength and dignity, reaffirming their existence even or especially in oppressive circumstances.

1. Interview Adnan Musallam by author, Bethlehem, August 2009.

3

A Land of Testing

"Every time I think about my country, Palestine, a few things pop out in my mind to explain why it is very difficult to live here, especially in Bethlehem."

Speaking is Susan Atallah, an English-language teacher at St Joseph School in Bethlehem. She is a prominent figure at the school, often seen in colorful dresses and wearing a bright smile. Her English is fluent due to her studies in the US. It is autumn 2000.

"The Holy Land is a land of testing. It's a land where your faith, patience, courage, and hope are all put to the test."

Or alternatively, where people's sumud is all the time being tested.

Susan Atallah: "When friends from abroad come to visit, they often ask us how we manage to live in a country where nothing comes easy. To get what you want or be who you want to be, especially as women, you have to be a fighter. This is why I encourage courage and confidence in my teenage students. I want them to set goals and pursue them. They need to have strong self-esteem and express their opinions without disrespecting anyone. They are learning to adapt to the current situation without accepting it as normal. Our lives and circumstances are far from normal, but we must find ways to cope."

Close to Al-Hussein Hospital in Beit Jala, Susan Atallah, known to everyone as (Miss) Suzy, heard a disturbing story from a shopkeeper. A family car was stopped near the village of Al-Khader, and the father and his three sons were ordered to exit the car and crawl on their arms and legs, barking like dogs. The middle son refused, and he was brutally beaten.

The shopkeeper shared this story with Suzy. Ismail, a school principal from Al-Arroub refugee camp near Hebron, shed light on the purpose behind such cruelty. Making the father perform such acts in front of his children is deeply humiliating, particularly in Arab society where a father's honor is central to family and community life. Furthermore, in Islam, dogs are considered unclean animals, so demanding that they imitate a dog is a highly degrading form of humiliation.

Addressing "moral dilemmas" is a method Suzy uses to create tension and engagement in her classroom. She posed a scenario to her 11th-grade students: if there were twenty people in a lifeboat that could only hold ten, what would they do? She also asked how they would react if asked to bark like dogs. The students affirmed that they would never comply. But when Suzy asked what they would do if their father was threatened with a gun, many of the girls admitted they would comply—given the circumstances, what other choice would they have?

Suzy enjoys challenging her students with these moral dilemmas. In another Bethlehem school, the Frères (de la Salle) School, teachers used to pose the question of what students would do if they encountered settlers who were lost in the desert and without water; a modern application of the Good Samaritan parable. During an auditorium session with around five hundred students, one boy claimed he wouldn't offer water to the settler since they were his enemy. Most others objected, arguing that this went against the principles of both Christianity and Islam. They insisted that helping those in need was the right thing to do. A clever student even came up with a political compromise, suggesting, "Okay, I'd give water, but then I'd organize a press conference afterwards."

"That water dilemma is trickier than it seems," remarked a lecturer at Bethlehem University, "because you know the colonists will later steal your water."

At St Joseph's, Suzy asked her students to consider reversing the situation. What did they think the settlers would do if Palestinians were without water? Unsurprisingly, the students didn't trust the settlers as much as they trusted themselves.

These moral dilemmas of today are not theoretical; they highlight the vulnerability of people in their everyday lives. In response to the story about the family forced to imitate dogs, one girl in Suzy's class began crying uncontrollably. She was related to a local Fatah leader who had been assassinated in a helicopter attack just two weeks prior. Known for her strong opinions and vengeful feelings, she often hears her father remind her, "Choose your words, lady." Beneath her opinions seemed to lie a suppressed fear and sadness.

※

During a storytelling session in a Bethlehem classroom in December 2000, a participating student steps forward indignantly, saying, "This part needs to be changed!" The story includes a sentence that suggests Israeli shootings and shelling are responses to Palestinian stone throwing. The student objects, saying it appears as if stone throwing initiates the conflict and shootings are merely reactions. Others counter that stone throwing and shootings are incomparable in their effects. The student argues, "But there's a reason behind the stone throwing too!" Someone suggests, "The occupation." "No, that's too general. In Al-Khader, soldiers forced a boy and a girl to kiss each other in public; that's why boys there started throwing stones." The students revise the script once more.

The next day, Mary heard a similar story from a cousin in Beit Hanina, north of Jerusalem. Her cousin's daughter, traveling by taxi from Jerusalem to Bethlehem, was stopped at a checkpoint. The soldier informed the seven passengers that they could only enter Bethlehem if a girl in the taxi (luckily not her daughter, as the cousin noted) kissed one of the men present. At first, she refused. The soldier then threatened that all passengers would have to stay there. The girl who was designated to give the kiss had an exam at Bethlehem University that she couldn't afford to miss. "I consider you a brother," she told one of the men in the taxi and gave him a quick kiss. After that, they were allowed to proceed. The soldiers were well aware of how sensitive public displays of affection are within Arab society, particularly between unrelated men and women.

I occasionally say to Jara, "Think of passing the checkpoint as a civics lesson. A lesson in real life, beyond the classroom. Notice how the Israelis treat you when you're with your Palestinian mother. It's quite different from when you cross the checkpoint with your Dutch father. It's like an academic experiment. In the first scenario, you might even have to take off your clothes when the X-ray machine beeps. Soldiers might yell at you and your mother. But when you go with your father, suddenly you're seen as a Dutch child: 'Ahhh... the Dutch are friendly and civilized,' you can almost see the soldier thinking. They just wave you through."

A Land of Testing

To lighten the atmosphere in class, teachers share funny incidents from the day. One Bethlehem teacher recounted how she and other Palestinians accompanied Greek Orthodox officials in a van on the way back to Bethlehem. At the checkpoint, soldiers were checking for permissions to be in Jerusalem. Most of the group didn't have the necessary permits. A little skit was put on to make everyone seem foreign. The officials, with their beards and long black robes, animatedly conversed in Greek with the Palestinians, who responded with gestures and nods, appearing to agree wholeheartedly. Another Palestinian passenger stared vacantly at the van's ceiling. To complete the scene, a large dog in the car started barking. Frustrated, the soldier didn't know how to react and just waved the van through. About twenty meters down the road, the passengers burst into laughter.

※

One of Suzy's projects at the time (2001) encouraged her eleventh-grade students to conduct oral history interviews within their families.[1] The results were striking and were compiled into a book. These girls' oral histories recount family events as remembered by the elderly. They describe moments like during heavy bombing in the 1967 war when a fridge suddenly opened, causing food to fall on a guest's head. There's also a story of a pet dog being hit by a shell or women preparing artichokes for the first time but being forced to flee midway through the meal.

The stories become especially poignant when they relate to the Nakba, the flight and expulsion of Palestinians during the 1948 war. In two separate instances, students recounted family members carrying a reluctant grandfather away from their house. A particularly moving story revolves around Beit Safafa, a village near Jerusalem that was divided by the Jordanian-Israeli border before 1967. A large fence with railings was constructed to separate the two parts of the village. During a wedding procession, family and guests found themselves walking together yet apart on either side of the fence.

Another story is deeply touching. A grandmother who lived in Jaffa during the 1948 war wanted to retrieve her baby boy from her neighbor's home. She discovered that the baby had been taken away during the turmoil. She managed to secure a job as a servant for the Israeli family who had adopted the baby, appropriately named "Moshe" (Moses). This tale

---

1. See Atallah, *Your Stories Are My Stories*.

mirrored the biblical story of Moses, who was found by Pharaoh's daughter near the Nile and raised by his real mother disguised as a servant. Eventually, the mother succeeded in reclaiming her baby and returning home. The student who recorded the story found it difficult to sleep afterward.

One surprising discovery after reading around fifty oral histories is that these stories seem to reflect more the history of Palestine rather than just Bethlehem. Surprisingly, over half of the stories have origins outside of the town. While only a few students live in refugee camps, many have families that originally hailed from other places: Gaza, Ramleh, Jaffa, Ein Karem, a village that was destroyed, and even an area in Turkey where the Ottomans persecuted minorities. What ties these stories together is the tragic theme that defines the shared Palestinian experience: separation. Separation from the land and belongings, from family members, and from each other.

Paradoxically, the act of retelling the histories seems to overcome the wounds of separation, forging a connection across generations. What resonates most in these stories isn't solely the descriptions of past events, but the dynamics of the conversation between the young and the old. Several students share that their history-telling sessions at home often began during power outages caused by shelling. In the darkness, what else can you do but share stories? The common suffering and fear create a closeness, and in many cases, both the students and the grandparents rebuild their relationship, with the students gaining a deeper appreciation for the elderly and the elderly finding relief in the chance to share their stories.

Suzy refers to this as the "unbroken chain" forged through storytelling. It brings about a measure of trust and hope. In the words of one organization involved in her project, Wi'am – Palestinian Conflict Resolution Center (Wi'am meaning "cordial relationships"): "In a time when so much is being systematically taken from the Palestinian people, we feel the need to light a small candle of hope instead of cursing the darkness, for we know the dawn is coming."

※

In 2001 Suzy has also initiated a diary project with her eleventh-grade students, and it's proving to be a success.[2] Last week, German TV visited the school and filmed one of the girls. The segment showcased her reading her

---

2. See Atallah, *The Wall Cannot Stop Our Stories*.

diary, singing in front of fellow students and in the church, studying, and even doing aerobics at home.

The students at St Joseph's School appreciate Anne Frank's diary, and I've been asked to bring five more copies of the book from Jerusalem. The students at St Joseph's identify parallels between their own experiences of confinement and Anne Frank's life hidden away in the Amsterdam canal house. Their interest might stem from Anne's strong character as well as the confined circumstances in which she lived. Suzy has noticed that diaries or biographies of individuals with resilient personalities help her students develop their own inner strength.

At St Joseph's School, the diary project had a significant impact. Many of the eleventh graders continued to write in their diaries during the curfews of 2002. However, some stopped due to fear that the soldiers might use their English language diaries as evidence against their families. In a country with a history of occupation, there's an inherent reluctance to put things in writing. Suzy was especially pleased to have collected over forty computer diskettes containing these diaries. One teacher commented humorously: "*ya'tik al'afia*" [May God bless your health, an expression said to somebody who is at work].

Nadine, a *tawjihi* [matriculation] student, shared with Suzy that she had so much to write about, but she felt unable to do so. Her family was confined to one room in their own house while soldiers occupied other parts. She needed something from her room which was taken over by the soldiers. She asked permission to go there and she saw a soldier sitting at her computer. Ann Frank's book was on the shelf over the computer. He asked her if she had read the book. She said, "I read it and I think you need to read it!"

The teachers at the school are now using the diary project as a means of helping students cope with the traumas they've experienced. Many students are grappling with a deep sense of meaninglessness. They wonder about the point of studying and going to school when life is devoid of enjoyment, with no foreseeable future, no prospects for normal university studies, no travel opportunities, and no job prospects in a collapsing economy. Some entertain thoughts of death and vengeance against their enemies. Others suppress their feelings and avoid discussing their experiences, turning away from the news as well, which they find boring. This, the teachers note, can lead to internal pressures and emotions building up to an *im*plosion. Some students even feel guilty for having experienced less violence and deprivation than those living around the Church. They refuse to eat, feeling it's unjust when others are hungry. Yet others startle at the sound of a school bell or a slamming door, fearing soldiers are entering the building.

❦

Suzy points out that the current challenge in teaching is finding ways for students to express their anxieties. She assigns the students to write "a letter to an Israeli soldier" or to comment on a drawing of a big fish eating a smaller fish eating an even smaller fish. The big fish sees the world as fine, the smaller fish see it as partly fine and partly problematic, while the smallest fish views the world as a disaster.

❦

Suzy herself is also facing challenges.

Living not far from the Church of the Nativity area, she shares the difficult circumstances she and her family are enduring in the first curfew of 2002, while the Church of the Nativity is besieged. They are without electricity, and even when there is power, she cannot enter her own room because it's unsafe. Instead, she and her family huddle in the bathroom and kitchen, listening through the window to the shouts of soldiers in the nearby streets. If the soldiers approach, their house might be searched, and they must rush to open the door, as not doing so could result in it being blown up.

In her neighborhood, close to the besieged Church of the Nativity area, tanks roam the streets firing indiscriminately. There are few people outside. The firing is more about intimidation than anything else. She recalls a terrifying moment when gunfire erupted from all directions, and she and her family members scattered within the house, each seeking refuge in a different room, calling out to each other to come together. During a recent window of relative safety, as she was leaving her house, she found herself face-to-face with a sharpshooter on a nearby balcony. The standoff was brief but felt like a lifetime before she cautiously continued on.

The feeling of living under siege has led to a sense of impending death for many. Suzy mentions typing a diary entry from a matriculation student at St Joseph School. The student's thoughts revolve around themes of dying and burial, with Bethlehem depicted as a dead place where people

A Land of Testing

are trapped alive within their own homes. The siege of the Church of the Nativity is especially painful, as it symbolizes both pride and vulnerability. Everything from homes and services to land and religious symbols feels threatened. Even a friend and neighbor who remains in Jerusalem due to work expresses her mourning by refusing to change or buy new clothes.

☙

Suzy's observational skills extend beyond the classroom. She has a keen eye for the interactions between students and their parents. In March 2003, she notices George Sa'adeh, a parent, picking up his daughter Christine at the school gate. Their interactions are charming, filled with jokes, and it's one of those small daily encounters that can bring joy to family life. Suzy has seen Christine grow up as a good and happy student since kindergarten. George, known to Suzy's colleagues at the Institute for giving computer lessons to students involved in exchanges with Dutch and Flemish schools, is a familiar figure. The day is a seemingly normal one, though conversations are dominated by discussions about the war in Iraq.

On a Tuesday early evening, tragedy strikes the Sa'adeh family. George Sa'adeh, his wife, and their daughters Christine and Marianne are driving through Bethlehem when they are caught in the crossfire of gunshots. The gunfire comes from an Israeli army unit in civilian attire who are targeting Palestinian militants. Unfortunately, they also fire upon the Sa'adeh family's car, mistaking it for the vehicle the militants are in. Some sources suggest that local informants had provided incorrect information to the army, leading to this mistake. Israeli media report a slightly different sequence of events, claiming that the militants fired at soldiers, who then returned fire, hitting George's car.

The incident occurs in downtown Bethlehem during the early evening, when there are fewer people on the streets due to heavy weather. Among the bystanders, at a distance of about a hundred meters, is Dutch Franciscan Louis Bohté, who lives in the Nativity Church complex. He later realizes that he has narrowly avoided being hit by a stray bullet. When Suzy is contacted that evening, her voice is heavy with emotion. Israeli TV broadcasts show images of the exploded passenger bus believed to have been targeted by the militants.

This incident is termed an "extrajudicial execution" by human rights organizations. Such actions involve the killing of individuals without any form of legal process, leading to "collateral damage" like the Sa'adeh family and other bystanders who happened to be nearby. Since the beginning of the Intifada in September 2000, at least ninety-six militants and forty-two bystanders have been killed. The international community, including United Nations Secretary-General Kofi Annan, has strongly criticized these actions due to their lack of due process and the risk they pose to innocent lives.

The tragic death of Christine has a profound impact on the community. Her burial is scheduled for Thursday afternoon. All the girls and teachers of St Joseph School form a long procession, dressed in their uniforms and accompanied by scouts with drums. They walk towards the small gate of the Church of the Nativity. As they arrive, the Muslim call to prayer echoes through the mosque loudspeakers, followed by the ringing of church bells. The voices of some young people chanting political slogans gradually fade, leaving an atmosphere of solemn silence broken only by the rhythm of the drums. The procession carries a large colored picture of Christine and a sea of flowers. Banners with messages in both Arabic and English are held high, bearing sentiments such as "Christine, you are our messenger in heaven," and "Christine, you will always be in our hearts."

At the conclusion of the procession, some participants carry a Palestinian flag that extends several meters in length. The estimated presence of around two thousand people show the widespread support for Christine and her family. Due to limited space inside the church, many, including myself, have to remain outside. After the prayer service, a group of men lift the coffin above their heads in the customary way observed by both Christians and Muslims. I blink back tears as the sunlight breaks through the clouds after weeks of heavy weather. A compassionate priest expresses his distress, questioning the absence of divine intervention and angelic protection.

Following local tradition, for the first three days after a death, friends, acquaintances, and sympathizers visit the grieving family's home. Separate rooms are designated for men and women. This practice has become more frequent due to the difficult circumstances arising from the Intifada. The emotional strain, coupled with economic hardships, has resulted in a higher rate of deaths, especially among the elderly. Recently, my family-in-law's neighbor passed away, and I observed the rituals as my family-in-law hosted visitors. Customarily, a dish called *kiddreh* is served, consisting of herbed rice with lamb meat. Additionally, bitter Turkish coffee is offered in small cups, which is believed to alleviate depression. During the initial day of mourning, visitors sit quietly to provide support. As the days progress, conversations gradually resume, fostering healing and revitalizing the community. Sana'a, the principal of a UN school in a village near Bethlehem, showed me how, during a mourning period, Muslims bake a special type of crispy bread that is then broken and shared among family and friends.

❧

In the streets of Bethlehem, one frequently encounters posters bearing large photographs of individuals displayed on walls and shop doors. These posters memorialize *shuhada* [martyrs], reflecting the broader Palestinian interpretation of the term. Rather than solely implying a willingness to die for a cause, martyrdom in Palestine encompasses anyone who lost their life in the context of the national struggle. This includes those who happened to be near clashes or extrajudicial executions. Last week, Israeli mortar fire in Gaza resulted in seven deaths. Among the victims were a Hamas leader and an associate, while others, including two children, were bystanders who rushed to the scene and were hit by a second rocket.

Also Christine Sa'adeh, the ten-year-old girl who lost her life in an extrajudicial execution two weeks ago, is considered a *shaheeda*. Her poster, featuring her face alongside a cross and a Palestinian flag, is displayed on the streets of Bethlehem and near her family's home. Earlier this week, a delegation from the Institute visits the family. George, the father, appeared frail but was recovering. His wife's expression revealed the immense grief the family is experiencing. Clothed in black, the women sat together, their faces etched with pain and exhaustion. George sought our assistance in finding a reputable lawyer in Jerusalem. It seemed that he wanted to take some form of action, perhaps as a way to confront the overwhelming sense of helplessness.

Upon returning from the visit, I find myself unable to contain my emotions and curse the world. Why must such a tragedy befall a young family?

❧

A 17-year-old girl from St Joseph School shares in her diary last week: "I dreamt that I was walking along a dark road holding a small candle. On the right side, I saw Israeli soldiers beating a small boy, and on the other side, I saw myself throwing stones at an Israeli jeep. I didn't care and continued my way until I reached the top of the hill. There, my little candle blew out, and the sun rose above Bethlehem, which was as green as grass."

During a teacher workshop in 2004 which focuses on diary writing, participants note that Palestinians in the region have become less strict about adhering to customs such as refraining from hosting wedding parties for up to a year after a family member's passing. While in the past, such customs were strictly followed, the current frequency of negative events has led to a more flexible approach. As Mary says, one has to live.

When some of the St Joseph girls are invited to the Institute to discuss their diaries, they reveal that they have learned to compartmentalize their emotions in order to focus on their studies. They recognize the need to distance themselves from the death and destruction surrounding them in order to concentrate on their exams and diplomas. Diary writing sessions at school, led by Suzy, provide an outlet for these repressed emotions. Sometimes, the girls break down in class while sharing particularly difficult stories, and Suzy herself is moved to tears in front of the students. She encourages the students to balance these moments of despair with positive thoughts and actions as life continues.

During the workshop, students present scenes from theater productions they've created based on each other's diaries. Despite the heartbreaking subject matter, they show enthusiasm and talent in portraying these stories. One student reenacts Christine's death by dramatically falling down in front of the class, as Christine was the sister of one of her classmates. This student aspires to become a theater director.

Some of the diarists refer to themselves as "sweet sixteen," but they grapple with the question of what is truly "sweet" about their lives.

Suzy's projects may not be indicative of the broader state of Palestinian education. In a conversation in 2010 with my colleagues Fuad and Walid at the Arab Educational Institute, we discuss Palestinian education and a project involving Christian and Muslim students learning about each

A Land of Testing

other's religions. I inquire about how changes in students' attitudes might be assessed at the beginning and end of the year. Walid, an experienced teacher at Bethlehem University, sighs deeply and laments the state of Palestinian education. He highlights the lack of enthusiasm among teachers, low salaries, overwhelming syllabi, and doubts about the effectiveness of their efforts.

Fuad shares a metaphor he heard from an acquaintance comparing education to preparing *mahshi*, a delicious Arabic dish where vegetables are emptied and filled with a mixture of rice and lamb. Similarly, students' minds are cleared and stuffed with knowledge, but even insightful elements in textbooks are often memorized without deeper understanding. This mechanistic approach undermines critical thinking, comparison, and independent judgment. Both Walid and Fuad express concern.

Palestinian education, as they describe it, is struggling. Knowledge acquired is quickly forgotten. Fuad mentions that children at the Institute no longer remember the names of refugee camps around Bethlehem, and teenagers aged sixteen and seventeen don't recognize the name "Balfour" or understand its significance. This lack of historical knowledge affects their ability to engage with the Palestinian cause. Fuad laments that many children nowadays are more interested in computers, pop music, and online interactions than in learning about their own history and culture.

The term "Facebook generation" is commonly used to refer to the younger generation that has grown up with access to social media and the internet. At a workshop, the difficulty of recruiting volunteers for various tasks is discussed, and it's noted that traditional forms of engagement and volunteering are becoming less popular. Scouts and other volunteer opportunities are struggling to attract participants. The allure of the internet, social media, and digital entertainment has shifted the priorities of many young people.

Nafez, from the Library on Wheels organization in Hebron, observes that while interest in reading physical books is declining, there are still pockets of enthusiasm. He mentions that in rural areas around Hebron, borrowed books are read extensively until they fall apart. However, in more urban areas like Hebron and Bethlehem, the rise of the internet has reduced interest in reading. Fuad predicts that when the internet becomes more accessible in rural areas, the same trend of declining interest in reading books will likely follow.

Suzy's role-play activity at St Joseph's involves a scenario at the airport where students must decide whether to leave or stay. This mirrors a real-life dilemma experienced by many Bethlehem families, known as the "sumud dilemma."

As summer arrives, familiar faces return to Bethlehem, visiting from abroad. The mixed feelings of leaving and returning to Bethlehem are captured in the words of Mary's niece: "Everyone who leaves Bethlehem behind looks good," but upon returning, "It is the most beautiful place in the world and you do not want to leave." This sentiment is echoed by others, highlighting the emotional complexity and attachment people have to their homeland despite the challenges they face.

I see Jara deeply concentrated in the books. This year she is looking forward to reading books more than during previous years. In fact, there are hardly any subjects that she dislikes. Tamer learns an Arabic poem this morning by heart, about how Saladin won a battle. With difficult, ancient words, in classical Arabic. He likes it. He pronounces the words well, says Mary. But afterwards he goes to the computer to play Star Wars.

4

The Mad Permit Game

"Why don't you go to Tel Aviv and enjoy yourself instead of insulting and humiliating the Palestinians? You took Jerusalem away from us, and now you also won't allow us to move around Jerusalem. Who are you to take away this right? You know you're in a place where you don't belong! Shame on you and on Sharon! My family and I shouldn't have to climb the hills like fugitives to avoid you. How can my mother do that?"

It is summer 2004. The soldier at the Wadi Nar container checkpoint, east of Jerusalem, had asked Mary, her mother, and her sister to open their luggage, but then he didn't allow them to continue their journey, at least not on that road. Another soldier accompanied him, whispering something in his ear. Mary was sure he was warning the first soldier to ignore her. In the meantime, Jara was crying. Afterward, she told Mary that she was afraid the soldiers would shoot to keep Mary at a distance. "You know, Mama, I love living in Bethlehem, but I hate Sharon and his soldiers!"

In reaction to the traveling obstacles, Mary said, "Now we're like slaves—slaves without even the right to shout at our masters." "How sad is it that we're happy to receive a permit," she said upon hearing about people who were granted permits to travel to Jerusalem during Easter week 2005. She applied herself but didn't receive one. We heard about many couples who were given only one permit. According to some, there were seven hundred permits to distribute among a thousand applicants. Most people didn't bother applying.

November 15, 2005 is Palestinian Independence Day, though there's of course no real independence. I decide to take a break and visit the zoo

The Birthplace of Jesus Is in Palestine

in Jerusalem with the children. Mary, who can't join us due to her lack of a permit or a foreign passport with a three-month visa like mine, packs things in the bag for me and the children. Should we include a knife in the bag to cut fruits? It's better to have a plastic knife instead of a metal one, we think, since the soldiers at the checkpoint might get suspicious.

I do a quick check on the Internet to see if there are any issues expected on the road. The Bethlehem taxi driver informs us that today the new terminal is operational. As we approach, it's not a checkpoint but something resembling an international border. People heard it was going to open soon. Irony prevails as it happens on Palestinian Independence Day. Surely, no coincidence. As if the message is: If you want your independence, we're glad to grant it by creating an international border and confining you.

I count four inspection moments. First, at the gate in the Wall, where a soldier checks whether I have a passport. I wave it. Then we enter through iron corridors into the terminal itself. We pass a glass booth where a soldier quickly checks the passport. A Palestinian woman wants to enter a revolving fence but doesn't have a *tasreeh* [permit]. A rather loud-speaking soldier on the other side of the fence denies her entry. The kids and I pass through, somewhat overwhelmed by all the iron and cement around us and the immense size of the hall. It reminds me of *Eretz* checkpoint at the Israeli entry to Gaza.

Months ago, I read in an Israeli newspaper about an army representative who stated that the new terminal would allow people to wait quietly, shielded from heat or rain, and that toilet facilities would be available. Indeed, we pass male and female restrooms. Everywhere there are huge signs urging people to keep the place clean. The hall is a blend of iron revolving gates, corridors with high roofs, and large and small signs. We wait for a few minutes in front of another revolving fence with a red light atop it. Through the fence, we observe a Palestinian trying to comprehend the Hebrew-spoken commands of a female soldier. She seemingly wants him to remove his belt. Or is it his shoes?

She communicates via a loudspeaker from behind glass. The loudspeaker is exceedingly loud, causing echoes due to the hall's size. It feels like cattle rather than humans are being inspected. Not entirely, though, because of the cleanliness emphasis. However, I reflect, modern cattle facilities are also quite clean. I wonder what this place will look like after a few months.

Another woman joins the queue. She giggles nervously. Typically, people waiting at checkpoints are either angry or passive, but the iron, technology, and vastness here must make them primarily feel out of place. Jara starts panicking because we forgot the bag of apples, and now she thinks soldiers will question us about carrying a knife without fruits. The light turns green, and we pass through the revolving door. The soldier lowers her voice upon seeing me and Jara, with Tamer on my arm.

I recall that long ago, Mary used to attempt to enter checkpoints with baby Jara on her arm to lighten the soldiers' mood. That now seems like an almost romantic past. There's no way to talk your way through this place. I place my belongings in my bag, which is X-rayed. "Don't bring your hand too close to the bag," the soldier cautions. She's perhaps instructed to be stringent during this first day of the terminal's opening. Jara is relieved the plastic knife remains concealed in the bag. Through the loudspeaker, the soldier bids me, "Have a nice day," but it's far too loud. This is the third time we've heard it, I reckon. Everything is askew here, both in place and proportion.

Then, we proceed to inspection point number four. The passport slides through the glass window and is meticulously examined from all angles. "Have a nice day," we hear again, mechanically. We exit the terminal, feeling relieved. Jara tugs my arm and whispers in my ear that she spots a soldier relieving himself behind a pillar. She giggles and asks why he's doing it. Don't they learn to use a restroom?

On the way to the zoo, Jara gasps at the greenery lining the roads. "How beautiful it is here!" she exclaims. As we walk through the zoo, a comparison with the terminal can't help but come to mind. The zoo's various sections are small-scale, human-oriented, diverse, and clean. The play area features imaginative stone animals with two heads and other whimsical attributes. Animals roam freely in the children's zoo. You can breathe here; there's no tension. When there are Israelis beside me observing the animals and Jara and Tamer are shouting in Arabic, I feel slightly tense, as if this isn't the right place to speak Arabic loudly. "Don't think foolishly," I tell myself.

However, this time there seem to be more Arabic-speaking visitors in the zoo. In fact, the zoo advertises itself as a meeting point for Jews from various backgrounds as well as Arabs—Arabs from Jerusalem and Israel, that is.

I recall a conversation I had about half a year ago with Sana'a, the headmistress of a school in the charming West Bank village near the Israeli border, Battir. Part of her village is slated to end up on the wrong side of the Wall, caught between the Wall and the invisible Green Line that separates the West Bank from Israel. She mentioned that the Israelis had approached Palestinians to offer school classes in her village the opportunity to take the train that passes through the village once a day to visit the zoo. It seemed like a kind gesture, but I suspect it was mainly for propaganda purposes and photo ops; a way to show that Palestinian kids affected by the Wall don't suffer excessively. Frankly, I understood the negative response. Palestinians need rights, not favors.

On the way back from the zoo to the Bethlehem terminal, the Israeli taxi driver informs us that he can't turn on the meter (which calculates the time/distance of the ride and determines the fare) because the area near the checkpoint isn't considered part of Jerusalem's boundaries. It's a ploy to extract more money. I catch myself arguing that at least according to Israeli law, the checkpoint area is well within Jerusalem's boundaries, and therefore he should activate the meter. I feel ludicrously hypocritical; after all, both the zoo and the terminal are located on the lands of Beit Jala and Bethlehem; West Bank lands, not Jerusalem's.

Then we head back home through the terminal. I engage in small talk with the soldiers to ease the tension for the children. As we pass through the Wall gate, I glance back and see an enormous mural on the Wall. It portrays an American lion covered in dollar signs and oil installations, devouring a Palestinian lamb. The next day, I hear from Palestinians that they waited at the new border for 1,5 hours and that tourist groups were segregated from Palestinians. Bethlehem will soon be encircled by the Wall on three sides—north, south, and west—with the desert to the east.

☙

I have now had firsthand experience with the new-style Israeli checkpoints, particularly the Bethlehem and Qalandia terminals. The following list of observations is taken from my notebook:

1. Initial Impression: The overwhelming feeling is one of ugliness, particularly at Qalandia. You traverse sand dunes, concrete roadblocks,

The Mad Permit Game

nine-meter high sections of the Wall, watchtowers looming over the Wall, steel and wire structures, military installations, turnstiles, desolate parking lots, makeshift garbage dumps, and ongoing construction for hundreds of meters. Pedestrian pathways are hardly present. It's as though you're approaching the edge of the world. Bethlehem's terminal is a bit more organized and cleaner—likely due to the presence of tourists—but it too is cold and unattractive in design.

2. High-Low Effect: At the Bethlehem terminal, soldiers walk on iron scaffolds above you. They look down upon you, making you feel both observed and insignificant. To see the green lights that signal where you can pass, you must crane your neck upward. Are there soldiers in the watchtowers rising above the Wall? You cannot tell. The glass is opaque.

3. Labyrinthine Structure: Without a stream of people to follow, it's often unclear where to go. If no green light is visible, which line should you join? Yesterday morning, I stood with a group of people at the Bethlehem terminal, shouting repeatedly, "Hello! Is there someone here?!" An observer from the World Council of Churches Ecumenical Accompaniment Program, stationed at the terminal, called a guard on his cell phone. "YES... THEY'VE BEEN WAITING HERE FOR 15 MINUTES. NO, NOT THAT LONG YET. THEY DON'T KNOW WHERE TO GO." The group and I found another entrance behind the concrete barriers and encountered a soldier sitting there. She must have heard everything but remained seated, immobile.

4. Cattle Comparison: In both Bethlehem and Qalandia, the experience of passing through numerous fences, pens, and barred corridors gives one a sensation of being treated like cattle.

5. Unpredictability: A common trait of both new and old-style checkpoints: you never know how long the wait will be. Even if only a few people are ahead of you, the wait can unpredictably stretch out. I've been fortunate so far.

6. Lack of Eye Contact: In the Bethlehem terminal, you pass through three or four checkpoints. At the first post, the soldier often dozes with their head resting on the table. You can't see them clearly through the window. When you go through the gate and the metal detector beeps, they wake up and call you back. At the X-ray screening, the soldier is barely visible, hidden behind dark glass. At passport control,

soldiers frequently sit and converse with each other or engage in phone calls, leaving you waiting without acknowledging your presence. A colleague mentioned that at the Eretz checkpoint in Gaza, soldiers often make eye contact—either friendly or confrontational. In Bethlehem and Qalandia, being ignored is commonplace. You simply do not exist.

7. Technology: Complete with beeps, push buttons, and lights. As expected, the technology often malfunctions or works excessively well, such as when the X-ray machine continues beeping even after you believe you've removed all metal items.

8. Language: Soldiers often address Palestinians, tourists, or visitors in Hebrew, even when you're speaking English. Don't they learn English at school? They do, so there's more to this practice. The late Maha Abu Dayyeh, a leader of a women's rights and advocacy NGO, once told me that Palestinians speaking Arabic at checkpoints can be a form of subtle nonviolent resistance.

9. Border Impression: The terminals are vast and give the impression of permanent border crossings. However, they are situated on occupied territory.

10. Hypocrisy: Upon exiting the border post towards Bethlehem, you'll notice a massive banner draping over the Wall beneath a military watchtower with the slogan "Peace Be Upon You," signed by the Israeli Ministry of Tourism.

In an interview shortly after the Wall was erected in the Ramallah-Jerusalem area, the mentioned Maha Abu Dayyeh succinctly captured its impact:

> One must realize how the Wall, specifically, and the overall living conditions psychologically obstruct us. When you are psychologically obstructed, your thinking becomes restricted. Your capacity for creativity is hindered. Your capacity to experience emotions is hindered because you must constantly shield yourself from frustration. It's a form of psychological torment. You're always on alert. You can't relax. You perpetually consider how to tackle the next obstacle. You can't ever plan and anticipate completing a single plan. You must always have plan A, plan B, plan C. Often, the goals you've toiled so hard for remain unattainable. Disappointment is a constant companion.[1]

---

1. Interview Maha Abu Dayyeh by author, Jerusalem, December 2004.

The Mad Permit Game

She speaks about an anger which she feels is essential for Palestinians to resist. For her, anger is part of a lifestyle of resistance-for-dignity, or, as one might say, sumud:

> My anger means that I am alive. My anger makes me act more, be more constructive with my colleagues, with my kids. I try to help them cope with the situation they are in. Being able to use my anger to help others is important to me because it gives me energy. If I can maintain my anger at a steady level, I am energized. Anger means that I am trying to act on what happens. I think people need to be angry all the time about the situation. People have the right to be angry and express their anger. It's a sign of living, a refusal to die. Some people just choose to survive because they are tired of resisting and fighting; I can't blame them. I consistently hope that not all people in our society fall into that mode. So far, it looks like they are resisting and fighting.[2]

Jara says that only in heaven there are no checkpoints.

She often plays checkpoint at home. She stretches her leg across the narrow corridor to block Tamer and me from passing. She holds my zoo entrance card between her outstretched middle and forefingers, mimicking soldiers' aloofness. She scrutinizes my card for a while, occasionally glancing at me to check if the photo matches. Tamer joins in the game and lets me through only after I jump up and down in front of him. The children enjoy giving orders to daddy. I attempt to outmaneuver the checkpoints with quick sprints, utilizing alternate doors.

Mary is exasperated: "Did you know that the scanner confiscates and retains jewelry at the checkpoint? Where do you think those jewels end up?" In the Christmas season 2006–7 more and more stories emerge from people who had to remove rings and earrings, placing them in the plastic tray, only for these items to disappear into the machine, never to reappear. Mary lost a ring half a year ago that I had given her. The soldiers offered no assistance in recovering the lost item. You can leave a telephone number, but then you never receive any follow-up. Last week, a friend of Mary lost

---

2. Interview Maha Abu Dayyeh by author, Jerusalem, December 2004.

an expensive earring. Last week, when soldiers took someone out of his house in a village east of Bethlehem, almost ten thousand dollar vanished from the house. Just rumors?

Mary describes a dream where she is sitting in a car with Israeli soldiers. In her dream, she tells a soldier that a slow murder like the one Palestinians are enduring is more difficult to endure than a swift death. "Is that truly your opinion?" I ask. She laughs enigmatically and shrugs.

Unexpectedly, many Christians in Bethlehem receive a one-month permit to visit Jerusalem and Israel. Not only during specific hours from eight in the morning to five in the afternoon, as is typical, nor a permit to visit a designated place or hospital in Jerusalem—no, an open permit. Astonishing. Mary's relatives rub their eyes in disbelief. A ticket to freedom? Mary: "It's disheartening that you have to feel joy at seeing your own country. You are being subjected to doses of air, much as animals in a zoo or inmates in a jail."

That sense of being imprisoned is reinforced by the construction of a hundred-meter-long corridor lined with high barbed wire along the Bethlehem side of the Wall. This corridor was erected a few months ago after Muslim pilgrims were denied access to Jerusalem on Fridays during Ramadan, leading to clashes at the gate. Back into the prison you go. I ask about permits for the Muslim holidays at the year's end. Nobody knows for certain.

Sometimes Muslims over the age of forty-five are permitted to go through the Gate, but this only applies to Muslim Palestinians from specific cities and is subject to relatively unpredictable moments. Suddenly, the word spreads that passage is allowed. People attempt it. Then, out of nowhere, long lines of individuals are waved through. "*Ruuh, ruuh*" [go, go]. Jara adeptly mimics the gesture, waving her hand.

We have a one-month permit to go to Jerusalem. The Israelis might have issued this "generous" permit for Christians to deliberately sow divisions between Muslims and Christians. A friend of Mary recounted an incident from last week at the Allenby Bridge. She was singled out by a soldier from a long queue. He called her forward, saying, "Come here, you're a Palestinian Christian, you're not against us, come on, you can pass!" She wished the ground would swallow her up. It was dreadful. She felt like she was being presented as a collaborator for all to see.

The Mad Permit Game

April 2007: Mary shares her recent checkpoint experience with me at the end of the day:

> Today, I went to the checkpoint with Jara and Tamer, after obtaining my Easter permit from the parish. As usual, we had to place our rings and jewelry in the basket. Jara also removed her bracelet. She entered and exited the X-ray machine several times, each time removing something new, but the machine kept beeping. Then the female soldier behind the bulletproof glass instructed her to take off her pants. In public.
>
> Would you let your daughter undress like that, with everyone around? I said to the soldier, 'Why can't you conduct a body search?' She refused to leave her glass booth. And I refused to leave. Jara was crying; she didn't want to remove her pants. She's now old enough to feel the humiliation. I stood there for 15 minutes, going back and forth between closed iron doors.
>
> The soldier wouldn't allow any of the waiting people to enter. It was like a showdown testing our wills. She told me to go back to Bethlehem. I retorted, 'You have no business here; you go back to Tel Aviv yourself.' I became furious. The last time, when I was there with my sister and her son, I remained very calm. My sister and nephew became nervous after we couldn't find my diamond ring, which got stuck and lost in the X-ray machine. But when it's your daughter, it's different. I told the soldier, 'I hate the way you treat me!' And then I insulted her and her government with words I can't bring myself to repeat.
>
> *Ya rabbi* [my lord], how angry I was. Wouldn't you be? No, I'm certain you would remain composed; that's your nature, and of course, you're a foreigner. You don't feel the humiliation. What I despise are those orders shouted at Palestinians: '*ta'al!*' [come], '*ruuh!*' [go], '*islah!*' [take off]. So the soldier refused to let me in. I turned back and passed by the twenty-five or so people waiting, and they asked me what happened. I recounted the tale, and they responded, "Oh yes, of course, insulting them means you can't enter."
>
> What should I do—bow to them? Let people pass there naked next time, with journalists present. Let's show them how inhuman they are. To comfort Jara, who was crying again because we couldn't proceed, I assured her we'd tell her story to the world. Tamer asked me, "Did Jesus hear?" I reassured him, "Yes, he certainly did."

We approached another soldier elsewhere and explained the situation. He was taken aback and thought we should be allowed to pass. He returned to the female soldier behind the glass, who falsely gestured that I had spat on her. But of course, I did insult her. He then patted Jara on the back, attempting to console her. I became even angrier and told him, "Don't touch my daughter!"

But I was determined to go to Jerusalem. In that moment, I didn't want to give them the satisfaction of denying me entry. So I tried my luck at the DCO [District Coordination and Liaison Office] in Beit Jala, which is open for foreign passport holders but not permit holders. I went there with my Chilean passport. I was even ready to pay the driver fifty shekels for the trip.

The chubby female soldier at the DCO was in a good mood. Even the driver, who knows her, joked with her about how she could be in such high spirits after serving there non-stop for a month. She simply advised me to bring the Dutch passports of the children next time.

So we went to the American Colony in East Jerusalem, looking for Easter eggs. Jara was happily playing outside. When we entered the courtyard, guess who I saw? Israelis sitting with their guns beside them, just like that. Is anyone asking them to put their weapons away or go through the X-ray? Why do they have the right to carry arms in my country, even in a hotel, without anyone questioning them?

Deep down, I think I'll never ask for a permit again. Why should we go to the mall [the large shopping center in Al-Malha in Jerusalem near Gilo]? To support the Israeli economy? I believe it's a mistake to get a permit. Many people can obtain permits these days, but they refuse. I think they're right. The humiliation is just too much to bear.

Given that sumud is the refusal to relinquish one's human dignity, there are various Palestinian counter-practices at checkpoints. These include employing tactics to pass through or avoid the checkpoint—examples of small victories necessary to uphold one's sumud. Not complying with everything the soldiers demand, expressing disagreement through subtle gestures, or small acts of challenge or disapproval, are typical forms of resistance that I've observed. Clicking one's tongue, refusing to speak or understand Hebrew, maintaining an angry expression, or even holding a direct gaze

The Mad Permit Game

with the soldiers to assert an equal footing are common ways Palestinians challenge authority.

Women often have more space to engage in such challenges, particularly against male soldiers. A practice that might seem like passive acceptance—waiting at the checkpoint—can actually contain elements of opposition. Jara once suggested to Mary that she should dye her hair blonde so she would face fewer problems at the checkpoint. But Mary responded, "No, I'm Palestinian, and I'll remain so." The thought "To exist is to resist" crosses my mind. It's a slogan gaining more traction here.

However, humiliation can always worsen.

After returning from a trip to the Netherlands in spring 2008, I find myself back at our familiar Bethlehem checkpoint the next day. It's almost as if the checkpoint has become a welcome familiar sight. "The checkpoint welcomes you home," a Palestinian once ironically said to me. The loudspeakers above emit a cacophony of squeaks and roars, directed at the waiting crowd. Is that the same singer again?

A few weeks back, I was waiting in line with Tamer and Jara among a group of Christian Palestinian drivers who had permits to enter Jerusalem for a few weeks due to Easter. Boredom had settled in as we stood in the queue, when suddenly a soldier in the booth behind us started putting on a performance. "*Irja, irja*" [go back], she sang out to the people passing through the X-ray machine. I tried to explain to Jara that sometimes soldiers do strange things, even behave strangely. Today, that same song again. The soldier keeps repeating "*irja, irja*," first slowly, then faster, higher, lower, shorter, and ending in crackling screams. Could she be losing her mind? People in the line exchange concerned glances. "*Majnoune*," someone mutters—an insane person. When it's my turn, I raise my passport. Initially, she motions for me to go back, but then her expression changes as she realizes I belong to a different category, a foreigner. Her stubborn demeanor morphs into a smile, and I'm allowed to pass.

A German volunteer, a theologian who's working here, shares these checkpoint experiences. He's begun writing them down, as have observers from the World Council of Churches and Israeli *Machsom* [checkpoint] *Watch*. From his notes, I learned that it's not uncommon for soldiers to belch into the loudspeakers. In one instance, a middle-aged woman was made to go through the X-ray machine between fifteen and twenty times (the volunteer lost count). Every single time she went through the gate, the soldier would call through the loudspeaker in what seemed like a friendly tone: "Welcome to Israel, the best country in the whole world." And then, when ordering her to go back: "Thank you for visiting Israel." The woman was in despair because she didn't know what to do. In the end, it turned out that the beeping came from the needles in her headscarf.

☙

But the pinnacle of absurdity was reached at a checkpoint in Al-Arroub camp.

In 2003, I was an instructor for an intensive diary-writing course in the refugee camp of Al-Arroub, north of Hebron. Ismail, an UNRWA school headmaster, and I used to walk several kilometers along the main street of the camp because the lecture halls we used were spread out. Every few meters, Ismail would greet people sitting in front of their houses and shops. He claimed to know almost everyone—at the time perhaps around 3000—inhabitants of the camp by name. Even amidst the crowded refugee camps, the ties between people are strong, though sometimes influenced by family tensions or political divisions. At the end of our daily walks, after dozens of polite greetings and declined invitations, we'd reach the camp's entrance, where Ismail would flag down a taxi for me. There, we'd naturally increase our pace.

Saying goodbye in such a place feels incredibly awkward. On the other side of the main Jerusalem-Hebron road, the army has erected a gray cement watchtower, about 15 meters high. On top of it, there's a dark, semi-circular narrow opening from which soldiers peer out over the camp. It's hard to discern whether there are soldiers in the tower or not. Every morning, as Ismail sets out from the camp to go to work in Hebron, he and his driver must stop in front of the coiled lines of razor wire blocking the entrance. Holding their IDs high, they wait until soldiers, using binoculars, finish their inspection. A metallic voice from the tower then asks who Ismail is, what he intends to do, and where he's headed. The same questions are directed at the driver. Ismail suspects that the identical questions, asked each morning, come from the same soldiers, but he can't be sure as the metallic sound of the loudspeaker renders their voices unrecognizable. The soldiers might know Ismail, but he doesn't know them.

The Mad Permit Game

The most challenging part of this surreal interaction between technology and human being is when Ismail holds his ID up but is uncertain if there's a soldier in the tower. Standing in an unnatural, frozen stance, he feels foolish. Questions swarm his mind. How long should he keep his ID raised? Are the soldiers perhaps mocking him by not appearing, or are they truly absent? Is this a test? Would they open fire if he moved the wire and asked the driver to proceed without permission? Ismail says he's found himself waiting like this several times. After about two minutes, the sense of humiliation becomes too overpowering, and he moves forward. So far, he hasn't been shot at, but what about next time? Passing the watchtower obstacle always brings him relief. In extreme cases, it can take up to twenty minutes. Needless to say, this isn't his only travel obstacle. On his way to work, Ismail goes through no fewer than six checkpoints. These increase his six-kilometer journey to downtown Hebron, where his school is located, to an average of 1,5 hours.

During one of our regular meetings, Ismail showed me his own diary. On that particular day, he'd woken up at four in the morning and couldn't sleep. He wanted to document his Via Dolorosa and share his daily experience with the world. "Do you never get angry?" I asked him. He responded with a smile, remaining silent.

✲

Visitors to the West Bank often wonder why people here remain so calm despite the constant humiliations, frustrations, and delays. I believe it's primarily due to adaptation. A week or two ago—it is 2008—the Israeli army conducted raids in the 'Azza refugee camp in front of our house for three consecutive evenings. These operations seemed aimed at apprehending individuals who had expressed their frustration by throwing stones or Molotov cocktails toward the military watchtowers surrounding Rachel's Tomb near the Bethlehem-Jerusalem checkpoint. One evening, we heard a sound bomb; the next night, as I strolled in the garden, a faint scent of tear gas reached my nose. These raids typically occur in certain districts and camps of Bethlehem, usually out of sight of tourists and cameras. I can't help but feel a sense of guilt for my numbness, my outward "calmness," while just a few meters away, people are being taken from their homes.

It's the routine of occupation. The everyday occupation[3], as highlighted in the title of a recently published book on the subject. The magnetic

---

3. See Makdisi, *Palestine Inside Out*.

card is a prime example of this routine. Mary, after much internal struggle, decided to obtain that card from the army's administrative headquarters at the Etzion settlement near Hebron. She did so in order to ensure her ability to go to Jerusalem at Christmas, when permits are available at the parishes. She was prepared to swallow her pride. One thing she knew in advance was that Bethlehem residents came on Mondays; other cities and regions had their designated days.

But don't imagine signs with waiting times and guidelines, or a number dispenser. In the Israeli military bureaucracy, the rules are not fixed. The experience is Kafkaesque. In her innocence, Mary went with a friend at nine o'clock in the morning, a time when regular offices and shops open. The waiting crowd eyed her as though she came from another world. She learned that only women were given numbers; men were not. In reality, women had to queue from six in the morning. Some men were already waiting near the closed gates in a state of tension from three in the morning.

And then comes the next uncertainty: you have no idea when your turn will come. It's not like waiting in line at a bank where you can expect to be served after a certain wait. People sometimes wait for twelve (!) hours in a single day, from six in the morning to six in the afternoon, only to return home without success. There are instances where hundreds of people are waiting until, say, eleven o'clock in the morning, when they're informed that the office is unexpectedly closed for the day. (I've experienced this a couple of years ago.)

To my bewilderment, I hear from composed voices around me that there are individuals who make it their weekly mission to go to Etzion every Monday. My colleague knows people who have done this three or more times without any success, holding onto hope that they will eventually prevail. In short, people are treated as if they're not human. Self-respect dissipates. I ask those around me for more information, and they confirm everything I've described, but with an emphatic request not to include their names. Revealing their names could jeopardize their chances of obtaining a permit.

Mary tells me that I shouldn't forget to mention that Israeli human rights observers are occasionally present at Etzion. A cousin of Mary's colleague, who is a lawyer, experienced a situation where soldiers distributed waiting numbers to both men and women when these observers were around. But as soon as the observers left, the same soldiers collected those numbers again.

The Mad Permit Game

Once an acquaintance delivered a particularly rich speech while waiting for hours at the Civil Administration office in Etzion. All Gods and political leaders of the region were thoroughly cursed without exception. "What do you do in this damned country?" he asked Mary. "Go to Holland, stay there for two years, what are two years after all, get a passport and make a life." He kept his mobile open while the soldier with whom he tried to have contact on the phone conversed for more than twenty minutes with other callers. "Otherwise, they will tell me that I behaved rudely by closing the phone."

It is New Year's Eve, 2011. "*Ahhh ya* [oh] Toine," Mary says with a heavy heart. On the background sings the Lebanese singer Fayrouz her melancholically sounding Arabic Christmas songs. Mary received a Christmas permit for Jerusalem, but others in the family did not. She had wanted to go to Jerusalem with all her close family, especially because Mary's sister and her family from France are on a visit. Mary calls other family to enquire. The same problem: half of the couples or families got a permit, the other half not. Everybody is calling each other to learn who has and who doesn't have a permit, as if the lottery announces its prizes.

A few years later, in 2014, Mary says that from the very beginning it was not a good idea of the churches to become an intermediary or a kind of "facilitator" in the permit system. It was not good to comply with the practice to have Christian believers picking up Israeli permits in churches so as to be able to make use of what in fact is a fundamental right. "But I do understand why they did it. People need a little bit of air."

Mary closely studies the permit. She notes that it is for about a month and that it is only valid when specific conditions are followed, numbered 1, 2, 3, 5, 8, 9 and 10. One condition says that this particular permit can be used without a magnetic card. Another condition specifies that you cannot stay the night in Jerusalem, and so on.

But there is something else. Mary hears that also children below 16 years are receiving permits at the parish. "That would be the day," she says—the day when children need permits as well. "You know how they [the permit bureaucracy] are," says the parish secretary, "They sometimes do this, and sometimes that." Until now children automatically receive permission to pass checkpoints when accompanied by an adult who can prove their age.

A familiar ring echoes in my mind. About half a year ago, an incident occurred at the Bethlehem-Jerusalem terminal that caught our attention. Soldiers asked our daughter Jara (14) for a permit. At the time, we dismissed it as soldiers perhaps being in a peculiar mood.

However, upon reflection, it appears there is a method behind this chaos. Within the occupation apparatus, new measures are gradually and discreetly introduced, like the recent requirement for children to possess permits for Jerusalem access. These measures are tested sporadically and in various locations, preparing the public for their eventual implementation. The strategy involves generating confusion and ambiguity to gradually dull people's anger and resistance until the measure is openly declared and enforced. This gradual erosion of the connection between West Bankers and Jerusalem, ultimately turning Bethlehem and other regions into virtual prisons, showcases the insidious nature of Israel's occupation. It operates as a continuous process, sometimes overtly like the construction of the Wall, but often subtly and gradually.

A few years back, an educator at Bethlehem University explored the significance of "Jerusalem" to her students. She was taken aback when several students responded with a disheartening, "Nothing." The persistent closures had left them without a tangible understanding of Jerusalem, even though they lived merely five kilometers away from the city.

Jara's excitement is barely contained as she proudly displays her new, sizable permit with its intricate layout and text. Her friends have received similar permits—but not all of them. It's astonishing to think that now the permit system has even ensnared the hearts of children. Jara approaches me with a request to leave a permit beneath the flower plant in front of our house for one of her friends to collect. Families collect permits from the parish and distribute them among neighbors, friends, and relatives. Even Tamer (9) has received a permit, though he voices his protest, questioning, "Why do I need one?"

An article in *Haaretz* highlights the complexity of the permit system, revealing that there are a staggering 101 distinct types of permits utilized to control the movement of Palestinians within the occupied territories. These permits cover a wide range of scenarios, including attending weddings, funerals, medical appointments, court hearings in Jerusalem, and of course, permits for Christians and Muslims. Thousands of Israeli employees find employment within the permit bureaucracy. The article also notes that "[a]ccording to a report by the UN Office for the Coordination of Humanitarian Affairs, international agencies operating in the West Bank waste an estimated 20 percent of their working days on permits from the Civil Administration—applying for them, renewing them, and resolving issues related to them."[4]

Furthermore, the article adds that "The checkpoint-monitoring organization *Machsom Watch* claims that the Shin Bet security service uses the permit regime to recruit informants. Palestinians whose permit requests are rejected 'for security reasons' are often summoned to meetings with Shin Bet agents, who then dangle the prospect of 'assistance' in securing the desired permits in exchange for information."[5] The other side of this disturbing coin is that individuals are often hesitant to engage in nonviolent resistance, as they fear the repercussions of potentially being denied permits or being added to a blacklist.

FIGURE 2

Cars waiting at checkpoint 300 between Bethlehem and Jerusalem

4. Levisson, "101 Types of Permits."
5. Levisson, "101 Types of Permits."

5

Rhythms of Life

IN THE SUMMER OF 2001 I join a group of political visitors on a tour through the town of Beit Jala, which borders Bethlehem to the west. Our taxi driver, well-acquainted with the various targeted locations due to his involvement in providing relief to afflicted families, seamlessly transforms into an experienced guide. He meticulously distinguishes between holes caused by 200, 300, and 500 mm mortars. He indicates the spots where the *Tanzim*, Fatah-affiliated militants, used to take cover and fire; where the Israeli army launched its shells, and where the German medical doctor Harry Fischer walked, aided his neighbor, took shelter, was hit by a mortar, and lost his life.

These places now carry an intensified, almost timeless significance. As a guide, I'm accustomed to pointing out sites linked to the Nativity. However, there are now other guides who, with equal authority, reveal locations of suffering and death—a sort of modern-day Via Dolorosa. The visitors capture these scenes in photographs. The experience is disorienting, partly due to the serene hush that currently blankets the town. This tranquility stands in stark contrast to the memory of bombings and destruction. A certain calm seems to descend upon the Bethlehem area, perhaps attributed to the summer heat and the deceleration of life as the holiday season approaches.

Timelessness and pastoral serenity are inherent attributes of Bethlehem. The name of this town reverberates across the globe and holds unwavering meaning for hundreds of millions of people. Throughout the nineteenth and the first half of the twentieth century, numerous photographers—predominantly European but also Arab—endeavored to capture and possess this timelessness in their images. Local Palestinians, some likely compensated, posed as models for the Nativity scene and the shepherds receiving the good news. These pictures have rightfully faced critique for their inclination to excessively romanticize the image of Bethlehem. They transformed people into objects for a Western gaze, fixated solely on "observing" eternal Biblical scenes, whereas in reality, a thriving community was grappling to endure in the midst of conflict and occupation.

The timeless message of Bethlehem harmonizes with the rhythm of pastoral existence, attuned to the agricultural cycle and the manual skills characteristic of Palestinian traditional crafts. I've spoken with glassblowers and pottery makers in the region who shared how the rhythmic motions of their hands were acquired in their formative years and couldn't be easily learned as adults. It's analogous to how learning to play the piano is best undertaken at a young age. Some even posited that the kinetic aptitude for specific handicrafts was inherited through genetics.

My Arabic teacher Aida shares stories of her mother's vivid memories from the past, when she and the women of her extended family and neighbors would gather in the courtyard of their home. They would sit together, diligently working on intricate cross-stitch patterns that are characteristic of Bethlehem's embroidery. Glancing over each other's shoulders, they'd watch to see who was progressing faster, while their conversations flowed with the tales of the day. Their hands skillfully wove colorful pieces of art, and it's these scenes that the elderly recall when reminiscing about the good old days.

A few years back, I engaged in a discussion with students at Birzeit University near Ramallah about depictions of Palestine in Palestinian literature. We were struck by how writers, even in the very cadence of their language, conjured up the idyllic daily life of an undisturbed and tranquil Palestine. In one recollection of his youth in Bethlehem, Jabra Ibrahim Jabra, the author of the restless novel *The Ship*[1], affectionately recounts the orchards and groves where people would gather during harvest season. They would ascend into the trees and sing their refrains as they plucked the fruits, one "tree" rhythmically answering the sung queries of another. A passage from Jabra's life story that resonates deeply with me now describes his father just before the man's health began to decline. A tire accidentally rolled downhill in Bethlehem, and his father sprinted after it, triumphantly

---

1. See Jabra, *The Ship*.

The Birthplace of Jesus Is in Palestine

catching it in the sight of his son. In that moment, the son observed his father's vigor and strength. I often find myself chasing after Jara's balls, as they persistently threaten to tumble down the steep hill near my mother-in-law's house. Perhaps unconsciously, I seek to show her that her father remains spry and active, as if time itself stands still.

※

Sumud too contains an element of timelessness, in the sense of patience, steadfast patience.

Together with my Arabic teacher Aida, I read a local story about King Sulayman, the snake, and the mole. King Sulayman is King Solomon of the Old Testament. While the King is in Damascus, the snake and the mole wish to know why they are without legs and without sight. The King tells them that he will dispense justice only from his throne in Jerusalem. The mole and the snake set records in their haste to reach Jerusalem, arriving even before the King on his famous horse. The King points out that if they, without legs or sight, can outpace his horse, how much devastation they could wreak upon the world if they were granted their request? They were created as they are to safeguard the world from their excessive need for speed.

※

The serene rhythm of Palestinian life has been disrupted not only by the Nakba, wars, and settlements, but also by capitalism fragmenting a peasant economy and its accompanying way of life. The tranquility of rural living has been replaced by a tension that few manage to evade. On my way home yesterday, I overheard a conversation between two taxi drivers lamenting how their colleagues are all relentlessly pursuing money. Regardless of one's stance on capitalism and financial success, it to some degree clashes with fundamental cultural values. Many Palestinians appear uneasy with the associated "fast" lifestyle, as if experiencing a dual displacement, both politically and culturally. The driver taking me back to Bethlehem, with no other passengers apart from me, declines payment, as if for a moment he wishes to reject everything that has tainted Palestinian life. Essentially, people yearn for the return of the good life, even if just briefly.

On Christmas Eve, the patriarch and the subsequent procession solemnly traverse Star Street to the Church, seemingly underscoring the essence of Bethlehem's message. The profound values of Palestinian culture likely align with the principles of an uncomplicated life rhythm. I've lost count of how many times people have told me, "Don't complicate things!" This perceived transgression is somehow linked to hasty and thoughtless actions.

While Mary and I are seated in a taxi, a few women pass by gracefully but at a very slow pace. The taxi driver leans back in his seat, placing his hands in a relaxed manner behind his head, and comments that the women walk "like the Patriarch."

In Bethlehem, we celebrate three Christmases: the Roman Catholic or Western Christian (December 25), the Greek Orthodox (January 7), and the Armenian (January 19). One particularly cherished memory from all the festive occasions is seeing Jara, and later Tamer, proudly dressed in gray uniforms with ties and hats, marching amidst the scouts during the arrival of the Roman Catholic Patriarch in Bethlehem on December 24. The bands represent various Christian communities in the West Bank. Our neighbor succinctly remarks, "Nice to see other Palestinians." We relish the unhurried rhythm of the drums and bagpipes, along with the vibrant uniforms of the bands, against the backdrop of the fresh yet crisp weather. "They hit those drums really hard," I mention. "Yes," responds the neighbor, "it's a way for them to release their anger."

The sense of timelessness that Palestinians often feel isn't completely uniform, but rather punctuated by bursts of intense, dramatic emotion and impatience. Some of the most frequently used words in Palestine are the impatient *khalas* (stop it) and *yalla* (move on), which contrast with the equally common *istanna* (wait).

Recently, while waiting in a taxi, Mary and I observed a conversation peppered with those words between a taxi driver and a group of peasant women. They wanted to bring their large baskets and boxes of vegetables and fruits into the car but were hesitant about the price they were asked to pay for the space. An animated discussion followed, complete with gestures and raised voices. But before long, laughter broke out. The taxi driver assisted in loading the heavy boxes, saying to the women, "After I've loaded everything, I'll have a backache, and women will refuse to marry me." Later, when we had to exit the car, we had to climb and jump over the fruits. The driver playfully told Mary that a little exercise would do her good.

The Birthplace of Jesus Is in Palestine

I'll forever remember the scenes where Mary and Jara, both playfully acting exasperated with each other, call out *"yalla,"* indicating that it's time for Jara to come and eat. Jara, not interested in eating at that moment, responds with her own *"yalla,"* conveying that she hears her mother, comprehends the urgency of the situation, but has her own private reasons for not wanting to eat right away. It's not uncommon for people who want each other to do something to use a crescendo of apparent mutual agreement, shouting *"yalla, yalla!"* but remaining unmoved and continuing with their activities for a while longer. A certain stubbornness is undoubtedly a Palestinian cultural trait, closely tied to the concept of sumud.

The leisurely rhythms are contrasted by the brisk tempo of music. When I listen to the popular Arab music often played during summer weddings, its beats remind me of the galloping of horses. Jara once shared with me that she learned at school that true Arabian horses actually have an affinity for music.

During a vacation in Egyptian Sharm el-Sheikh, Mary, Jara, Tamer, and I witnessed a horse show. As the Arab horses entered the arena and skillful riders displayed remarkable positions on the horses, the audience became enthusiastic. Mary and the kids stood up and cheered "bravo" when the Palestinian flag was carried by one of the galloping horses. More than anything else, a running horse symbolizes freedom[2].

Countless times, Palestinian and Arab artists have projected their ideas of pride, freedom, independence, and revolution onto the wild movements of Arabian horses. Mary's parents and their family used to travel to Jericho to attend Arab horse competitions. The sight of horses galloping across desert landscapes invokes the indomitable spirit of the Bedouin.

Once, we observed Jara running alongside a galloping horse on the pavement. How strong and free she appeared!

⌘

With fondness, my Arabic teacher Aida shares a memory of her family's life before they fled in 1948 from the Musrara quarter in Jerusalem to Beit Jala. Her mother would visit Miriam's Hammam, a Turkish bath near Jerusalem's Lion's Gate that served as a gathering place for Muslim, Christian, Jewish, and Armenian women alike. These women engaged in pleasant

---

2. For an account linking horse-riding and the Palestinian "character," see Lorusso, "Palestinian Character."

conversations without any distinct "religious" or "national" divisions. On the eve of a wedding, the bride would be adorned with reddish henna in front of cheering women who clapped rhythmically.

In addition to the well-known melancholic Arabic songs, there are more joyful traditions where people rhythmically clap and sing to celebrate communal moments. Whether it's birthday or wedding parties, picnics, bus trips, house-building events, or the return of an imprisoned son, both young and old gleefully engage in collective clapping and singing. Although these moments have become rare, they haven't entirely disappeared.

2013: Many people in Palestine are profoundly tired, often exhausted. Where do they find the wellspring of their energy? Could the rhythms of life be a contributing factor?

Rana, a therapist in Jerusalem, shares her insight that people manage their energy in a way that ensures they always reserve a little bit for the next day. A British friend of mine writes to me that individuals in desperate situations draw energy "from the daily life rhythm of providing food, sharing meals, watering trees, tending to animals, laughing, storytelling, and organizing festivals." She observed this phenomenon in India. She mentions that baking bread embodies hope and vitality. "Bethlehem, after all, means the house of bread."

Perhaps it's the very rhythm of daily life—unhurried and occasionally impatient—that fuels sumud.

Beyond being a struggle against adversity, sumud encompasses a profound love for and attachment to Palestinian homes, land, and life. The rhythmic aspect of this attachment finds expression in communal practices and celebrations. Consider the preparation of meals, the communal sharing of food and drink during seasonal gatherings, the hospitality displayed at weddings and other festivities, and the customs within and outside homes—like casual conversations and news exchanges on balconies or in outdoor spaces. Think also of the rhythmic patterns associated with crafts, or even the cadence of people's steps and interactions on the streets, or the rhythmic dance of the *dabkeh* [Palestinian folk dance].

The Birthplace of Jesus Is in Palestine

In December 2019, during a tranquil morning, I waited for an Armenian Mass to conclude in the Nativity Grotto. Seated with other guests on the entrance steps, we were enveloped by the timeless atmosphere of Christmas through the slow, rhythmic singing of the priests below us.

Yesterday, on the occasion of her birthday, Mary and I attended a Mass in the small chapel of the Bridgettine Sisters near Nativity Square. Nestled within a labyrinth of old, narrow streets overlooking Bethlehem to the north, the chapel exudes an ambiance of silence and the soft sounds of bells, evoking the ancient rhythms of the town.

Afterwards, we are hurled back into the familiar flow of time. We find ourselves considering various markers that punctuate a typical day. Will the *ka'ek* man arrive on time so we can purchase his sesame bread before Mary heads to Bethlehem University? Yes, we indeed hear his distant call in the morning hush. Or we catch the sound of schoolchildren's voices as they head to school, providing a gauge of the hour. We sense the brisk footsteps of students rushing to exams at the university, sometimes studying from books they read while walking.

However, an unwelcome third rhythm always makes its presence felt: that of occupation. It disrupts the harmonious cadences of life, introducing uncertainty and menace that put people's nerves on edge.

During the Second Intifada, there was an instance when Mary, her sister Rita, the children, and I attended the opening of an exhibition at the Peace Center, situated opposite the Church of the Nativity. The exhibit focused on travel and Palestinian identity. At the center's entrance, a collection of wooden, life-sized passports was displayed, intended to draw attention to the array of IDs and passports that Palestinians carry. Having already traveled to different parts of the world, I couldn't help but wonder about the reactions of security personnel at Tel Aviv airport when they saw these oversized alternative passports being unpacked.

Inside the center, we encountered two video monitors positioned side by side—two parallel rhythms. On one side, you were invited to adopt the perspective of a driver freely traversing the settler roads in the West Bank; as you watched, a sensation of unhindered movement and freedom filled you, as if the world was yours to conquer. On the other side, you experienced the viewpoint of a driver navigating the rough Palestinian roads of the West Bank, hindered by obstacles. "Look, there's the Al-Khader checkpoint!" exclaimed a visitor, recognizing his own reality with surprise.

Despite the somber subject matter, the atmosphere was surprisingly uplifting. Conversations buzzed with life. "Events like these help uplift the spirit," Mary remarked.

6

The Gift of Home

WALID MUSTAFA, A GEOGRAPHY lecturer and former Dean of Arts at Bethlehem University, is affiliated with the Institute. I once conducted an interview with him regarding the meanings of sumud.

> Remaining in your homeland is not solely about sacrifice and suffering. Sumud is a way of life, not just for those living in the present, but for generations to come. It's about embracing the joy of living within this environment, on this land, among these people. Allow me to share a quote from a Russian poem: "For me, the homeland begins from the bench in front of our house, on the street where my grandmother and mother, along with other women, sat and discussed life's matters." Sumud is tied to the beauty of daily life. When you reminisce about your homeland, its beauty becomes a part of you. So, by practicing sumud, you're not constantly suffering; on the contrary, you're expressing your love for the land. Through sumud, we convey our strong desire to continue living in it, just as our ancestors did. This homeland has granted you, your parents, and your forefathers the gift of life and the gift of living. You should feel gratitude towards this homeland, and you should remain loyal to it.[1]

---

1. Interview Walid Mustafa by author, Bethlehem, August 2009.

The Gift of Home

FIGURE 3

Old city of Bethlehem

❦

Sumud has a time and a place element. Patience relates to the time dimension. Staying and keeping home relates to the place. Sumud often means a presence, inhabiting one's home and homeland.

But how comfortable are the homes in Bethlehem?

Bethlehem's houses are often breezy and lack central heating. However, the genuine old houses, constructed with large stones and small windows, are well-suited for both summer and winter. During the summer, these stones keep the heat at bay, while in the winter, they offer protection against the cold.

Similar to other Mediterranean regions, traditional houses are often painted in shades of green or blue—colors historically believed to ward off the evil eye. Green might symbolize fertility or simply evoke a feeling of coolness in a warm climate. The rooftop serves various purposes, from drying summer fruits to offering a space for picnics and panoramic views of the hills for those fortunate enough to own countryside dwellings. In one of our rooms, we have an ancient photograph featuring Mary's great-grandfather and his family standing on a rooftop alongside a sizable water jar.

The Birthplace of Jesus Is in Palestine

Many *qasrs* ["castles"] are still present in the countryside—ancient watchtowers where peasants conducted their harvests, told stories in the evenings, and accompanied their singing with rhythmic clapping. Sitting beneath a fig tree in the garden while savoring a cup of mint tea encapsulates the traditional image of a peaceful life in Palestine. However, during 1948, these *qasrs* were repurposed to provide refuge for Palestinian refugees.

House and hospitality hold great significance for Palestinians. A serene yet lively household, welcoming hosts, and plentiful food are highly valued. I recall my first visit to Palestine in 1980. While exploring the refugee camp south of Bethlehem, Dheisheh, which wasn't yet a common destination for foreign visitors, I found myself compelled to partake in three meals in a single evening. I was moved from one house to another, responding to the insistent invitations of *"kul"* [eat]. Uncertain of how to resist the insistent culinary offerings, I eventually succumbed to the pressures and delights of the situation. My mother-in-law, like many mothers-in-law in this region, would give me a stern look whenever I declined to eat, questioning persistently and curiously, "Why don't you eat? Why?"

Indeed, the term *"beit"* [house] from "Bethlehem" isn't just confined to the physical concept of a building structure. It encompasses the notion of a "living stone," a hospitable space, a symbol of fertility and productivity, representing bread (*lechem* in Hebrew) or meat (*lahme* in Arabic). A house is also meant to be alive with the presence of many children. (I've lost count of how often family and friends have encouraged Mary and me to have more children.) On one occasion, students from a school in Beit Sahour reenacted the Nativity scene. The student portraying the innkeeper deviated from the script, saying *"tfadlu"* (come in) to the visitors instead of turning them away. Opening the door in Palestine and across the Arab world is an ingrained custom that invites both friends and strangers inside.

The founder of the Bethlehem House, a small but fascinating museum near Nativity Square, once shared with me that she struggled to believe the Biblical interpretation that the locals of Bethlehem turned away the Holy Family, especially considering the possibility of them being distant relatives and Mary being pregnant and fatigued from a lengthy journey. She wondered if it might be more accurate that Mary gave birth not in an unwelcoming stable but in a grotto beneath a house, as many Bethlehem houses are constructed atop such formations. Could it be that there wasn't an "inn," but rather the visitors were led into a typical family home and directed downward, away from the bustling family gathering space on the first floor, to the cave-like area where the household animals were kept—warm and serene like a stable? She reached out to Benedictine Father and archaeologist Benoit, who didn't oppose her interpretation. In fact, Luke's *katalima* (2:7) in the Greek translation doesn't signify "inn," as it's interpreted in the West, but rather "guest chamber." The Old Bethlehem House now displays to its visitors a grotto beneath a conventional house, featuring a wooden manger at its center.

❧

In Palestine, and potentially across the broader Arab world, houses often remain incomplete. Owning a house, particularly one surrounded by land, is a family's aspiration. People save for extended periods to construct their own homes. A house becomes a life-long endeavor and a source of familial pride. Frequently, construction begins even when the necessary funds aren't entirely available. As the sons grow older and marry, they may establish new stories atop the original house or adjacent to it. During challenging times construction often halts.

It's not uncommon for house owners to leave their homes for extended periods, renting them out to others in the meantime. After accumulating some wealth, these owners often return to their homeland to enjoy their houses once again during the later stages of their lives. The parents of Jizelle, a former staff member at the Institute and a teacher, once moved to the United States without selling their house. Instead, they rented it out and some of their daughters remained in Palestine. They plan to travel back and forth periodically to maintain their American green card, which facilitates travel.

Arab houses don't conform to the finalized designs of Western architecture. A Bedouin girl from the Galilee delved into the topic of the *incomplete* nature of the Arab house for her master's degree in architectural design. She highlighted how Arab houses often have open-ended elements, like staircases leading to nowhere. An Arab house is a process, not a fixed product. This, she argued, doesn't diminish its architectural value; rather, it enhances it.

The destruction of a house is akin to the collapse of life itself. Demolishing a Palestinian family's home equates to destroying their very essence. In a casual conversation with a supporter, former Israeli prime minister Sharon remarked that if there were shootings from Beit Jala to Gilo, he wouldn't let blood flow. He believed that the Arabs cared more about their houses than images of wounded individuals. He stated that the Israeli army would enter Beit Jala and demolish houses, row by row if necessary, to halt the shooting.

A Palestinian intellectual once referred to Israel's policy of demolitions, stating that a Palestinian house is a "potential ruin," with the specter of destruction constantly looming over it.

In July 2004, I conducted an interview with the aforementioned colleague Jizelle, the teacher in Bethlehem. She aimed to capture the communal spirit of Palestinian life after returning from an overseas journey:

> I can't explain why, when I first returned home, I had this feeling that I just wanted to leave this country. Yet, suddenly, after three weeks of unpacking and dealing with the multitude of tasks that follow travel, I felt a magnetism here that drew me in. It's as if there's an attachment. I can't put my finger on it precisely. After all, you can only scratch the surface of your life. You don't know what lies beneath that surface. But there's a feeling that captures you, even if it's just for a moment. When you ask me why, I can't quite identify the reason. Initially, you think there's nothing to do here, and you can't endure your life any longer due to the myriad problems you face. Then, out of nowhere, something comes along [snaps fingers], perhaps a friend's smile, an old lady's word, a cup of coffee with relatives, or family coming to offer assistance. It might be our family life, or our friends. You can't pinpoint an exact answer to why you want to stay here. It's just an irresistible feeling. It's strange, but that's how it works.
>
> After this trip, when I was completely at ease with my family, friends, and our regular "prison life" [laughs], I thought: Why do I want to leave? I shouldn't. I may not have many options here, but I still have better choices than others. I have a job, I'm studying at a university, I have friends and a social life. What do we really need in life? Respect, the ability to sustain a household, and our friends. It's not that complicated.
>
> I once had a problem with my car, a minor accident. I called for help, and suddenly, three cars arrived, filled with guys—my brothers, friends—asking, "Are you okay? What do you need?" The guy who caused the accident even got worried, thinking I had brought all these people to confront him. It's amazing how they're there for you when you need them. Maybe family life is better elsewhere; I've never tried it, but I've heard my father saying that he doesn't see my sister in the US for two days, even though

they live together. She works odd hours; she studies at night and wakes up early. Financially, they say it's better there. But if you work tirelessly without enjoying life, what will happen after a few years? It's not easy when you're stressed. Sometimes, I just want to sit with my big family, have a cup of tea. When they ask me, "What do you consider a day off, a holiday?" After visiting six countries this summer, I say, "I'm completely free when I'm away from the world, in my pajamas, having coffee with my mom, with nothing to do. It's such a therapeutic feeling."[2]

During 2004 our house is situated near the 'Azza refugee camp mosque, so we hear the call to prayer, the *muezzin*, five times a day. Even though the sound is loud, you become accustomed to it, and we usually sleep through the early morning call. During the day, Tamer excitedly echoes "*akka, akka*" after hearing the phrase "*allahu akbar.*" He enjoys listening to his own voice reverberate. We know the Muslim sheikh who leads the call to prayer, as he used to help Mary carry vegetables during her pregnancy with Tamer after she finished shopping near 'Azza.

This sheikh is also known to our Christian neighbor, who would play the mouth organ during the silent curfews last year while sitting on his veranda. Our neighbor is intrigued by collecting Islamic prayer songs; he and the sheikh share rare cassette tapes of Islamic music. Since the melodies and rhythms of Muslim prayer music have not been written down since the time of Prophet Mohammed, numerous variations have evolved. Even here in Bethlehem, the prayers slightly differ from mosque to mosque.

Some Palestinian municipalities enforce the synchronization of prayer calls among mosques, like in Hebron. However, in the Bethlehem area, there is significant variation in prayer times among the mosques. This variation creates a unique effect where the calls to prayer seem to "wave" across the land. During sleepless moments, when you have the chance to hear these well-delivered calls to prayer against the backdrop of a silent early morning, the effect can be mesmerizing. It's as if the voices of the mosques are traveling across the entire country. Somehow, these sounds manage to evoke the undulating hills of Palestine, its towns, villages, and the eastern desert—as if the landscape itself is allowed to breathe.

---

2. Interview Jizelle Salman by author, Bethlehem, December 2004.

The Birthplace of Jesus Is in Palestine

In Palestine, sometimes your hometown or even your own home can feel ghostly, like a fading shadow that barely exists. Mary's cousin recently returned home for a visit after spending several years in the United States. When she entered Bethlehem in the evening, she had to take a familiar detour around Rachel's Tomb, now a large military compound with security zones. She was taken aback, exclaiming, "What is this? I didn't recognize the streets. So desolate. Where was I?"

The garden is an integral part of a Palestinian home. On Friday mornings in 2005, when Tamer doesn't have school, I joined him for an exploration of the garden, made even sweeter by the arrival of spring. We passed by a small sculpture of the Virgin Mary hidden in an artificial cave made of little stones. A few days ago, Tamer had recited the *abana ladi* [Our Father] prayer there; then he changed the key and spontaneously chanted "*allahu akbar*," the Muslim call to prayer that he had become familiar with because our house is close to the mosque.

As we walked, we heard the enthusiastic cry of "*ka'ek, ka'ek!*" which cuts through the morning air, encouraging people to buy a tasty type of bread covered with sesame seeds. It's usually sold alongside falafel balls, eggs heated in the same oven as the bread, and a bit of *za'atar* [thyme] wrapped in a scrap of newspaper. The vendor carries the fragrant bread on a wooden cart that he pushes forward or balances on a tray atop his head. As a joyful game, Mary and I used to lay Jara, and later Tamer, horizontally on our heads, playfully shouting "*ka'ek, ka'ek!*"

Our vendor, thinking that I might be an easier target as a foreigner, often slyly adds more *ka'ek*, eggs, and falafel than I order. Innocently, he charges me the full amount. Recently, Mary shared with me that the guards at Bethlehem University have nicknamed him "the crow" because his creaky shouts remind them of the bird that brings bad news.

As Tamer enjoyed his *ka'ek*, he watched a little cat that's fond of making elegant leaps across roofs and terraces. Following the cat's path, he wanted to climb down from a low wall in the nearby courtyard. He assessed the risk involved, but Tamer often seems a bit hesitant to explore things, perhaps due to the fact that during Mary's pregnancy with him, Bethlehem experienced a lot of shooting and shelling. His first few weeks of life were marked by extended curfews that brought fear to the area around our house and garden.

The Gift of Home

To help ease his mixture of fear and excitement, I took Tamer's hand and carefully guided him down from the rocks to a lower plateau with bushes and flowers. We followed a gently descending natural path that quickly became narrow. At first, he hesitated to continue, but his curiosity ultimately got the better of him. We took a big step across a narrow, deep gap and landed on a neighbor's house roof.

This little journey turned into an adventure because in this country, you often find areas in or between gardens that are not meticulously cultivated. These areas create an atmosphere of wilderness within the surroundings. On the slope we were following, a pattern of terraces divided the land into elongated steps, akin to descending a giant staircase. The edges of these steps were marked by small walls made of irregularly shaped stones. As Tamer and I walked, we discovered new vistas in a landscape not yet shaped by the Western desire to impose order on everything around us.

Our neighbor, recognizing us as we appeared on the roof, invited us to come down. The neighbor still remembered me from a few years ago when, during the long curfews, the normal University Road became unsafe due to passing tanks. I had to take this unconventional route to reach my family's home.

Tamer and I carefully navigated the rocky, winding stairs and were graciously invited to share the neighbor's food and treats: *looz* [almonds], now fresh and slightly bitter, and *ka'ak* and *ma'mul*, two cookies traditionally enjoyed during Easter shaped like symbols associated with Jesus' crucifixion—the thorn crown and the sponge that held vinegar. While Tamer explored the garden, the neighbor and I savored half-sweet black Arabic coffee, its aroma blending with the warm morning air kissed by the sun. This tranquil scene reminded me of the boundary-crossing nature inherent in this neighborhood landscape.

※

During my tours as a guide, I would often engage with tourist groups about the various components of a Palestinian (Mediterranean) home: the well and *taboun* [oven] outside the house, and the courtyard where women used to practice embroidery, basketry, and pottery while sharing news. One particularly engaging topic was the *rosanna*, a small opening in the house that led to the roof. In the early twentieth century, young men used to climb through the *rosanna* to avoid conscription into the Turkish army. During the first Intifada, they used it to evade Israeli soldiers' searches.

Maha Saca, a passionate advocate for Palestinian culture, runs a Bethlehem store that feels straight out of the Arabian Nights, featuring a wide range of Palestinian embroidery and heritage items. To celebrate the fifteenth anniversary of her center's existence in 2005, she organized an open-air festival with folk performances, poems, and speeches.

A delightful, fresh fragrance wafts from a corner of the triangular square where the festivities are taking place. Two women dressed in traditional attire bake flatbread in an oven and distribute it to attendees. The square is bustling with foreigners, including a sizable group of young people from Rotterdam and the surrounding areas of the Netherlands, as well as Palestinians. It strikes me that for Palestinians, these cultural gatherings serve as a way to experience a sense of national unity that has been strained due to the divide between Hamas and Fatah.

Observing the scene, I can picture how a century ago, grain would be transported from Beersheba to Bethlehem on camelbacks. Families would store flour near their homes and women would bake bread in traditional ovens shared with other families; small clay structures known as *taboun*, measuring around a meter diagonally and sixty centimeter in height. Just like at the water source, women would gather at the *taboun* to share the latest news.

In a separate corner of the square, the Dutch group claps and dances. At this moment, everyone is joyful, much like during the numerous weddings and family celebrations in the summer, such as when in 'Aida refugee camp people welcome a prisoner's return.

7

The Past in the Present

DURING AN EXPLORATORY VISIT to the occupied West Bank in 1979, before I began living there, my first impressions of Palestine left an indelible mark on me. Despite the poverty and crowded living conditions in Dheisheh refugee camp south of Bethlehem, I was taken aback by the warm hospitality and the apparent ease of Mediterranean life, set against the backdrop of beautiful spring weather. Accompanied by a group of energetic teenagers who welcomed me at the camp entrance, I enjoyed a leisurely swim in the nearby Solomon Pools, archaeological reservoirs partially filled with water of questionable quality. After a joyful time together, my perspective shifted drastically as I entered their homes.

In each household, every single item, regardless of its size, turned out to carry a political significance. The young people played a little game with me: I would point to an object in the home—a pillow or a painting—and they would recount the political story behind it. The central theme was the Nakba of 1948, when over 700,000 Arabs were expelled from Palestine, as well as the ongoing oppression they faced in their daily lives, such as midnight visits from soldiers.

Once I settled in Bethlehem, I gradually gained a deeper understanding of life within the refugee camps.

❧

In 2001, we move to our new house across from 'Azza refugee camp. Some friends express concern, saying, "But that's even closer to the shooting."

The Birthplace of Jesus Is in Palestine

While that might be true, the location is also conveniently close to Mary's mother and sister, and not far from Mary's workplace at the university. The move itself is made comfortable with the assistance of hired help and Mary's carpenter cousin. "How do I look with this *Katusha* [name of rocket]?" jokes a helper from 'Azza camp, carrying a rolled-up tapestry on his shoulder. Unlike the local custom, Mary wants to paint the rooms in colors. Our favorite spot is a balcony facing east, where we spend most of our leisure hours. We enjoy fresh fruits from Jibrin's, a thriving vegetable market owned by people from 'Azza camp.

'Azza refugee camp extends from our street towards the Paradise Hotel. Around 2,000 refugees, or their descendants, reside there in cramped conditions, living in multi-story gray-dark buildings constructed from humble materials. Last week, I had the opportunity to visit the camp's youth club with the help of a member of the Institute's youth group, Mohammed. He invited me in his characteristically light-hearted and slightly ironic manner: "So you're going to live next to the camp. Perhaps you've never been there. Allow me to do you a favor and introduce you to your neighbors." Walking through the camp, I notice only a few women wearing the *mandil*, a traditional headscarf. Palestinian camps tend to lean towards secularism, though they are politically more outspoken than towns and villages.

Along the walls are posters of martyrs. One poster shows the collaborator in the camp who, a few weeks ago, possibly under pressure from the Palestinian intelligence, shot his Israeli liaison. When Israel returned his body after several days, the family of the man and a medical doctor held a press conference in which they showed pictures of the mutilated corpse.

Together with my colleague Shireen, I attend a *dabkeh* dance performance of some of the camp youth, a project made possible by the Japanese peace movement. My experience with youth from camps and villages is that if they get a chance to join an activity, they do so with almost total devotion and discipline. Some of the girls can't keep a straight face and break into a smile while dancing. The dance and song themes are derived from the refugee experience and deal with suffering, liberation, and return. While watching, I suddenly become aware that what I am observing the Israelis would call "incitement."

In a neighboring club, youth are making a wall drawing representing the nuclear attacks on Hiroshima and Nagasaki. Why Hiroshima and Nagasaki, I ask, as if the refugees need to be reminded that things can always get worse? The project leader explains that the Japanese peace movement annually commemorates the day of nuclear destruction in different places in the world. During this year's remembrance day, the *dabkeh* troupe will give a performance at the Peace Center of Bethlehem. Later in the summer, they will showcase their skills in Morocco and Paris; if they are allowed to leave, of course. There is a computer lab in the youth club as well. The Japanese effort clearly makes a difference; the youth are encouraged to be active and try new things. On the bare walls hang a few welcoming posters of refugees that were especially designed for the occasion of the Pope's visit last year.

While watching the posters, I remember the countless images and photos of Palestinian refugees; their still faces betray weariness, renunciation, and bitterness. Years ago, when I conducted a study of the portrayal of Palestinians in western popular fiction, I found that many thriller writers assigned desperate Palestinian refugees the role of fanatic terrorists. They were attributed with an "explosive" mixture of traumatic experience, anger, and despair. In many of the narratives, the fact of their homelessness made them easy prey for political manipulation by evil conspirators. Rather than having their own story, they were thought to only be able to obstruct the story of someone else. Many novels depicted the refugees' facial features, especially their "hard" eyes, but did not give them a voice and humanity. The refugees were represented as both unsettled and unsettling.

While walking through 'Azza camp on a summer evening, you see people sitting outside in front of the doors and the shops, talking, narrating, and gesturing. The youth leader I meet tells me that the club's name is *Handala*. The name is that of a story-teller: Naji al-Ali's popular cartoon figure, a little child who observes and comments upon the distressful situations prevalent in the Arab and Palestinian world, such as political repression, exclusion, corruption, and neglect of the poor. As if to underline the embarrassment caused by what he sees, he is always depicted with his back towards the viewer. The facial features should be imagined but not seen.

The youth leader says that the refugees of 'Azza feel different from the other Palestinians in Bethlehem. There is not a great deal of contact with the native population, although, unlike other camps, 'Azza is completely surrounded by the town. But the very fact of being adjacent to Bethlehem town only serves to underline the contrast. The refugees are not at home.

Last year, some of the refugees from the camp joined a journey towards the village from where many of them or their ancestors come: Beit Jibrin, near Beit Shemesh in Israel. The Israeli authorities did not allow them to come close. In fact, many Israelis are haunted by the image of refugees wanting to return. Recently, an editorial of an Israeli newspaper said that perhaps the major reason why the Israeli public, including a large part of the peace camp, recently made a nationalistic turn in their political thinking was the return of the Palestinian demand of the right of return.

Silently above the camp hangs a kite, a mini airplane with two Palestinian flags at the rear. A symbol of national pride or the suspended possibility of flying away? With the youth leader, I discuss an old project proposal of our institute that aims, if nothing else, at least at people's minds flying away. Beit Jibrin is located on the historical road between Hebron and Beersheba, or, viewed from a regional perspective, between Jerusalem and Cairo. Once we thought about the possibility of reconstructing the route Jerusalem-Cairo as an educational project. Children would learn about what happened over time on that route, what the monks, traders, military, and refugees brought to move from place to place. Students would see pictures of the route, make exchanges with schools along the route, and, if at all possible, visit some of the places. Beit Jibrin (in Hebrew Beit Guvrin) is central on that route. It used to be a strategically located Roman town, with lands stretching from Ein Gedi along the Dead Sea to Ashkelon along the Mediterranean. Later on, it became an important Arab village.

Presently it is a kibbutz. The school where many of the parents or grandparents of our new neighbors used to study is now the kibbutz' administrative building. The value of the project we were thinking of would be that students would mentally rise above their present-day fragmented conditions to gain a broader view of history and geography. Right now, Palestinians from the West Bank can neither visit Israel nor the Gaza Strip. The project would rest upon the assumption that life may be imprisoned but one's spirit is always challenged to fly away.

※

2004: Mary is rehearsing homework with Jara. I am more than a little curious when she is memorizing the names of refugee camps located in Jordan, the West Bank, Gaza, Lebanon, and Syria. In general, I am happy as a parent with the way politics is treated in Jara's Arabic language lessons, which I also follow myself. Mostly, they are about animals and fairytale-like stories, but here and there, a credible political story from daily life pops up, such as a mother and child who go to an Israeli prison, wait there for four hours in

The Past in the Present

front of the gate, then are obliged to return without being able to visit the father. Whatever Sharon may say (recently he requested the Palestinian Authority to stop the "incitement" in the textbooks as an Israeli precondition for cooperation in the Palestinian elections), this is a very true story that many families experience. Not including politics in the curriculum is not an option because then you relegate thought and talk about politics just to the street and to the home. On the other hand, too much politics obviously does not match the fantasy world of the kids.

So I inquire with Mary how the issue of the refugees is dealt with in Jara's *wataniyyeh* [national education, one of the subjects]. It turns out that the chapter defines Palestinian refugees as those "who were obliged to leave their homeland and want to return." "But is there not something about the who, the where, and the why?" I ask. No, the rest of the chapter deals with names of camps and numbers of camps, which need to be known by heart. It doesn't deal with the refugees' story. Mary is filling in the blanks and tells Jara about how at the time when Israel was established, many Palestinians were driven out, how the refugees in 'Azza camp opposite our house first lived in tents and now in much too crowded houses. Why the shop at the corner is called Jibreen, and the camp sometimes Beit Jibreen, as the inhabitants come from a place in Israel near Beit Shemesh which was called Beit Jibreen and which is now called Beit Guvrin. I tell Jara how you can still see in kibbutz Beit Guvrin the ruins of the old Arab houses and that reportedly the old village school now serves as the local administration block. Are we feeding her with hate, denying the legitimacy of Israel, as Sharon would have it, an accusation we have heard not a few times? It doesn't look like it; Jara is rather happy that she is finished with the *wataniyyeh*, as she already knew that Israel never was a great friend of the Palestinians, and wants quickly to shift to the fairy tales of Grimm before she falls asleep.

But my own curiosity has not dried up, and I ask a well-known local social studies teacher to what extent the students get real information about significant events in the Palestinian narrative, like the events of 1948 or the massacres at Kafr Kassem in 1956 or Sabra and Shatila in 1982. "No, there is, in fact, very little in the Palestinian curriculum about such events." "Even not about Sharon's role in Sabra and Shatila?" "No, as far as I remember, Sharon is not mentioned, and if Sabra and Shatila are mentioned, it is in passing, not in the context of a Palestinian story of suffering and resistance." He himself teaches students from 14 years on, but he says he knows from colleagues that at other grade levels the situation is similar. "Any events that are incriminating for Israel, such as massacres, are barely treated or not at all. As far as national politics is concerned, you can say that Oslo receives due attention, but that too is at a superficial level." So what is the reason? He pinches and shakes my arm and says, "It's the US and Israel which set the limits of the curriculum. In terms of power, we are nothing!" So it is up to the teachers and the parents to teach the rest? "Yes, exactly, I try by myself to teach a coherent national story." He too is filling in the blanks. Fuad, at the institute, tells me to be cautious with the conclusions of one teacher and to first check out with more.

So I inquire about what a few other teachers think, and I hear similar things. A UNRWA headmaster says that apparently under financial pressure from the American Congress, some *wataniyyeh* textbooks were withdrawn by UNRWA, and that also military figures in Palestinian history like Abdel Qader al-Husseini (Arab leader in the war of 1948) and 'Ezzedine al-Qassem (a leader in the Palestinian insurgency from 1936-39) are not dealt with anymore in the books. Is it because al-Qassem is also the name of the rocket from Gaza and because the military unit of Hamas is called 'Ezzedine al-Qassem? It seems. Mary, in reaction, "But that's incredible. After all, when the children grow up, they hear about such persons through other sources. Why should we hide ourselves from our own history?"

It's a year later, 2005. Occasionally, I watch over the shoulders of Jara when she does her homework together with Mary. Not only to practice my limited Arabic, but also to see what she gets to learn. The civics is interesting. A year or so ago, Jara was learning the names of all refugee camps by heart. Ein al-Hilweh is in Lebanon, she exclaimed enthusiastically, Wahdaat in Jordan, Dheisheh is in the West Bank, Jabalya in Gaza. There was nothing about what Palestinian refugees were, about their expulsion, the war in 1948, and the creation of Israel. As if the refugees came from a black hole. Not exactly a way to get a clear picture of your past and identity as a people. You learn your history in a series of isolated names and facts, not as a story.

The new Palestinian curriculum, introduced gradually over the last six years, is not without international controversy. Almost always that controversy concerns passages in the Palestinian textbooks that are anti-Israel or could be interpreted as such. The debate already has a name among connoisseurs: the school book issue. Parliamentary questions are sometimes

The Past in the Present

asked in the Netherlands. The Palestinian Center for Curriculum Development has published several studies on its website that try to give a nuanced answer to the questions. There are also studies that ask firm questions about another, less-investigated school book issue: the anti-Palestinian nature of some Israeli textbooks.

But my own question is different. How much focus does the Palestinian curriculum give to Palestine?

At the end of November 2005, the YMCA East Jerusalem (Advocacy desk) and the Arab Educational Institute in Bethlehem organized a seminar on how Palestinian identity and reality are treated in the Palestinian curriculum. There were three main conclusions.

1. The curriculum is too full. I see this when putting Jara on the school bus with a full bag on her back. Teachers do not have enough time to give real depth to all the material, especially the material about Palestine.
2. The civics curriculum describes a rather ideal world. Full of indications of how things should be, but often without a connection to the daily reality in which children live: huge unemployment, lack of travel opportunities, and political violence.
3. The curriculum is vague about what is seen internationally as controversial events, such as the 1948 war.[1]

You cannot generalize. In spite of all this, Palestinian education has risen a good number of places on the international quality ladder, said the district head of the Palestinian Ministry of Education in Bethlehem recently.

Armed with a permit, Mary, her family, and some colleagues go to Ein Karem. That is a place southwest of Jerusalem, situated on the spot where, according to tradition, John the Baptist (the Prophet Yahia for the Muslims) was born, and where Mary, the mother of Jesus, met Elizabeth, the mother of John. Ein Karem—"source of the vineyard"—was populated by Palestinian Muslims and Christians before 1948. They fled during the war. Several families among them now live in Bethlehem and Beit Jala. I know, among

---

1. This would change in later years, with the coming of new editions of social sciences and civics textbooks.

others, the brothers Zacharias, named after the husband of Elizabeth, who continued their forefathers' crafts in Bethlehem and own an olive wood workshop. In our company is a family with a name ("Do not mention their name," Mary reminds me) that also refers to Biblical events in the village.

We visit a few picturesque churches. The weather is nice and calm. Tamer and Jara play. We go to the church of the birth of John the Baptist. Tamer throws himself under the pews. A Franciscan comes to stand next to him. This is clearly not allowed. Jara asks, "Is this the last church we visit?"

Yes, it is the last church. But the house of the mother of Mary's colleague is located in front of the church. We go there. It is strange for someone to see the house from where your family left because of the war and to which they were never allowed to return. I remember a number of anecdotes from Palestinians whose family fled in 1948 and who, after 1967—when it became possible to travel from the West Bank to Israel—visited their family homes. A Palestinian educator once described to me how the new residents told him that formerly "Christians, not Arabs" lived in the house. He was an Arab, so his family could not be the owners. The visitor stood perplexed.

The family accompanying us undergoes a mixture of emotions. Seeing the family home turns out to be a confrontation with their own roots and with the Other; it is familiar and alienating. You feel angry but also resigned, because what happened is so long ago. The family recalls memories. They point to the balcony from which once a pregnant woman fell, who was then wrapped by the family in a warm coat made of the skin of a slaughtered sheep. A traditional remedy.

Then suddenly a voice from the house. "Why did you leave?" it sounds. The residents of the house apparently recognize the family who also appeared here a few years ago. A question, an accusation, an excuse, meaning "if you would have stayed, I would not have been in your house right now. Leave your place and it's gone." The family does not say anything back. They are also perplexed. We look at the family house of the other family, Zacharias, beautifully situated in the hills.

On the return journey, the family tells us stories of how the families fled; how at the end of April 1948, the dead and wounded from the nearby village of Deir Yassin (where more than a hundred people were massacred by the Irgun underground led by former Israeli prime minister Menachem Begin) were led along Ein Karem, and how tensions then increased. The refugees were not allowed to return afterward. Unless with a temporary permit, as now.

The Past in the Present

"Are we not on the way to our *masir* [destiny]?" says Mary, recalling an Arabic proverb.

Years later, I read in my Arabic lesson about the life story of the Palestinian architect Suad Amiry as told in her well-known book "Sharon and My Mother-in-Law"[2] (she had issues with both). When I read the passage in which she describes the journey to see the house in Jaffa where her parents had lived, Aida, my Arabic teacher, became teary-eyed. It turned out she, as a young child, had lived in that same neighborhood. Later on, before the checkpoint regime made it almost impossible, she too had made a half-hearted attempt to see the parental home again. "But the Israelis [who live in the house] do not want anything to do with you." Suad's story reflected her own story.

❧

Once Abdelfatah Abu Srour, director of the cultural organization *Al-Rowwad* [the pioneers] in 'Aida refugee camp not far from 'Azza camp, told me about his understanding of sumud.

> We are not like marionettes who shake their heads in acceptance, kissing the hands of the international community for whatever they give us. It is our right to be here, not the right of a French Jew or a Jew from elsewhere to come here and claim the land. The refugees still cherish their right of return, still keep Palestine in their thoughts, still keep the symbols of Palestine. That is also sumud, not accepting a policy of despair, not accepting to forget our rights in a land or space that has been erased from the map.
>
> Names have been changed, and new Hebrew names have been given to villages, cities, and streets. But the Palestinians still remember their histories and they have children and grandchildren who too remember. Sumud is preserving the identity, the memories, the customs and habits, the popular arts, the attachment to the land, the values that make us human beings, across generations. It is about attachment to Palestinian embroidery, the meals, the hummus, falafel, *tabuleh* [Palestinian salad]—now misrepresented as the traditional food of Israel—as served during national, historical, or religious events. Preserving memory and history helps to keep faith in the future and to have hope.[3]

---

2. Amiry, *Sharon*.

3. Interview Abdelfatah Abou Srour by author, Bethlehem, February 2010.

The Birthplace of Jesus Is in Palestine

FIGURE 4

In 'Aida refugee camp

Photography and video are on the rise in Palestine, especially among young people. In 'Aida camp, Abdelfatah's Al-Rowwad Center gives photo and video courses to young people from inside and outside the camp. The first batch of students has finished the Images for Life program in 2008, and I view about fifty photographs in the big hall of the center brought together under the title "Look Who We Are."

'Aida camp, with over five thousand inhabitants, does not only deal with all the problems that refugee camps have, including unemployment, a serious shortage of water, problems with sewage and garbage disposal, and regular raids by the Israeli army. The camp is also bordered by the Wall, which gives it a desolate outlook.

The photos express humanity, dreams, and hope. What is immediately noticeable are the pictures about flying. Flying as a theme is well-known in refugee situations. There is a picture of girls in a gym class spreading out their arms like birds. There are several pictures of children playing with kites. Once I interviewed a Palestinian who said that where people elsewhere say that the "sky is the limit," for her the "Wall is the limit." Is it

The Past in the Present

a coincidence that these years Tamer is constantly imitating Spiderman, climbing an imaginary web? I do not know.

Despair is apparent in a photo of clothes hanging to dry on a line set over a pile of garbage: "My dream hangs between them." A picture of a stump of a tree has a text that runs somewhat like this: "I protect life in Palestine, but I cannot find my way."

Al-Rowwad Center promotes the idea of "beautiful resistance," and there are quite a few pictures showing the beauty of Palestinian cultural identity, such as photos of jewelry, prayer beads, and embroidery, and photos of traditional architectural buildings (next to destroyed houses), and dance movements. "I dream of a future that is as colorful as the colors of my clothing."

One photo particularly strikes me: it shows a traditional teapot in a dark cave. The comment next to the photo: "The traditional Palestinian way of making tea. This photo was taken in a cave in the village of Wadi Foukeen [west of Bethlehem]. An old man lives in this cave; his country is threatened by Israeli settlers, but he remains in the cave and stands up against the settlers' attempts to take over the cave. As he clings to the land, he also honors old Palestinian traditions."

A year later, Jara asked me why the Israeli army so often catches people near our house. It also happened next morning after a raid into 'Azza camp in front of our house. At three o'clock in the night, Mary and I were listening to the creaking walkie talkies of a few dozen Israeli soldiers. We heard a few series of three shots. After fifteen minutes or so, a boy in his twenties with hands on his back was taken into an army jeep. I had the impulse to go out, to show my presence. It was no more than an impulse. "Please keep that out of your mind," said Mary, "Do you think they care that you're a foreigner?" Shortly afterward, the cock crowed at the pet store across the road, followed by the call to prayer of the *muezzin*. The army operations usually take place before the morning prayer. At night, Bethlehem belongs to the Israeli army.

"*Haram*—oh poor one," says Mary, "It's always the young people they catch, and then those young people are blamed for leaving the country."

The Birthplace of Jesus Is in Palestine

One of the themes of the World Week for Peace in Palestine Israel 2015, convened by the World Council of Churches, is "It's time for the healing of wounded souls." I had to think of that phrase in relation to the Israeli town Beit Guvrin, to the south-west of Bethlehem and Jerusalem. It has recently become a World Heritage Site. Heritage is often a matter of politics and also of traumas left unhealed.

A year or so ago, the Palestinian village of Battir, which is closer than Beit Guvrin to Bethlehem and located in the West Bank, succeeded in gaining the status of a World Heritage Site. That status helped prevent the building of the Wall along the ancient Roman terraces there, at least for the moment.

The other newly chosen World Heritage Site of Beit Guvrin has been partially built on the remnants of Beit Jibrin. Part of (the children and grandchildren of) the refugees of Beit Jibrin live in 'Azza refugee camp opposite our house. Undoubtedly, they look with less tourist or archaeological eyes at the announcement that the place where their parents and grandparents used to live has become a World Heritage Site.

Besides giving attention to the remains of a Roman theatre, the heritage site is mainly presented as a Jewish site, underlining the Jewish roots in the land. But the former Arab inhabitants and their predecessors have, in their daily life, for hundreds of years interacted with the remnants of the many periods that one encounters at so many archaeological sites here. Isn't that a relevant piece of information, also for tourists?

During a Sunday in 2016, we embark on a journey to the Soreq caves near a *wadi* not far from (West-)Jerusalem. No permit problems this time. Tamer has a Christmas permit, and Mary is over 50 years old, no longer considered a threat. Though you never know how the rules work out at the checkpoint itself.

The taxi driver instructs me to pretend indifference and play with the phone when approaching the checkpoint. Never hold your passport in your hand, as the soldiers will surely check. Later, he advises us not to speak Arabic and also avoid discussing politics, even in English.

Meanwhile, we receive explanations from this taxi driver, a former history and geography teacher, about both present-day and pre-1948 life

The Past in the Present

in the area. After the cave, with its colorful stalactites and stalagmites, the driver guides us toward an area we're quite interested in: Beit Guvrin and Tell Maresha, to the south of Beit Shemesh. This area is the origin of the refugees of 'Azza camp and has recently gained recognition as a World Heritage Site. It's our first time visiting.

The driver points out the remnants of the old houses of Arab Beit Jibrin. The archaeological findings are interesting, sometimes even spectacular. Due to the nature of the soil and extensive stone quarrying, there are hundreds of deep caves in the area. These caves were used for habitation and various other purposes throughout history, including storage, burial, and even pigeon breeding.

In the site's explanatory materials, the Arab village is barely mentioned. There's no mention of what exactly transpired in 1948 or the present-day refugees. As we explore, we hear a loud explosion in the distance. "Gaza," says the driver.

He continues to show us around. "Here is the house of the *mukhtar* [village head] who collaborated with the Israelis. That's why his house was spared after 1948, as was the case in many other villages."

We observe that Beit Jibrin used to stretch out over many kilometers— a slightly hilly and mostly fertile area. On clear days, you can even see the sea from the hilltops. The natural beauty is abundant, and we learn about gazelles, eagles, and even a wolf. Before 1948, these fields were cultivated with wheat and barley. You can find and pick herbs like *za'atar* [thyme] and *miramiyyeh* [mint] everywhere. "Don't pick them, especially not along the road, or you'll get a heavy fine."

Palestinian refugees often speak of a paradise lost when reminiscing about the pre-1948 villages. "Paradise?" says the driver, "Look at the *khubeiza* [a mallow native to the Eastern Mediterranean]. With this, you can feed the whole Middle East."

The farmers used to be prosperous. Compare that to the situation of their descendants in 'Azza and 'Aida camps in Bethlehem. Just last week, a boy whose family is from one of the former villages near Beit Guvrin was killed by the Israeli army in a demonstration not far from our home.

The driver-teacher has adapted to reality and has actually formed friendships among Israeli farmers. These farmers used to hire Palestinian laborers from the West Bank, whether with or without permits. One of his Israeli friends owns a flower company, and we pay him a visit. The current laborers are from Thailand and approach us, though they seem to speak only Thai. I'm asked to bring special flower scissors from Holland, a country to which he also exports his products.

We're allowed to pick mandarins and lemons from the garden trees and are given a vibrant bouquet of flowers, free of charge. With the *khubeiza* and other herbs we've collected, we head back home. It's a week's worth of food. "Sad," Mary comments, "stolen land, stolen produce."

When Palestinians contemplate the idea of a shared identity, they grapple with the challenge of lacking a robust, compelling, and unified national narrative that frames the Palestinian collective memory. After 1948, was there a unifying narrative, or was it merely one of survival and victimization?

One dimension of sumud is the refusal to let go of Palestinian history and the rejection of the official Israeli interpretation of historical events.

However, the prevailing rote learning approach in education in Bethlehem and the West Bank presents obstacles to creating a coherent and explanatory narrative. The historical narrative has only been integrated into schools in the West Bank and Gaza over the past decade. After Oslo and the subsequent fragmentation of the Palestinian people and their identity, is there still a cohesive national narrative left?

In addition to its perspective on history—that it must not be forgotten—sumud functions as a fundamental element in any Palestinian historical grand narrative. It expresses the connection to the land and the determination and endurance of the people in the refugee camps. It signifies resistance against colonization and the commitment to preserving identity. With its deep attachment to the land, sumud opposes ethnic cleansing and settler colonialism that continuously threatens the Palestinian people's presence on the land.

Simultaneously, sumud facilitates connections to smaller, subnational "micro" narratives. It resists an overly dominant master narrative, emphasizing everyday stories within and across communities, embodying the slogan "existence is resistance."

In 2007, during a workshop, I asked Palestinian youth leaders if it was possible to compile the thousand facts and stories that together form the overarching Palestinian narrative. Their response was an unequivocal yes. However, they stressed the need for context in specific stories. They favored tangible stories with a universal message of hope, creative resilience, and compassion. Stories of women were highlighted. While the Nakba should undoubtedly be included, so should the vibrant Palestinian society from the past. The social narrative is just as vital as the national one. "We must understand the cultural life in Jaffa before 1948, the visit of the renowned Egyptian singer Um Khaltum to Haifa, and the agricultural life in the countryside. Only then can we truly comprehend the extent of our national loss."

Those stories too are part of the historical identity of Palestinians. They are more like stories of popular culture or neighborhood history. One of sumud's educational challenges is to explore and construct the personal and community stories in interaction with the national story, as well as in interaction with the global stories of decolonization elsewhere in the world.

THE BIRTHPLACE OF JESUS IS IN PALESTINE

8

Good Morning, Dignity

COMPETITIONS ARE HIGHLY FAVORED here. Years ago, Bethlehem artisans successfully worked on creating the largest piece of embroidery ever made. The goal was to earn a spot in the Guinness Book of Records and garner some extra publicity. A similar event occurred in Nablus, in the northern West Bank. There, they crafted the largest piece of *kanaafeh*, a dessert made from yogurt and sweet flavors for which Nablus is renowned. The dessert was spread out over a table spanning more than seventy meters during a grand celebration. Those who managed to approach the tables could receive a free piece.

Among other heartwarming moments in recent history were when Palestinian artists won TV music competitions.

28 August 2004: The Palestinian singer Ammar appears to be an introverted individual. On the Lebanese Future station, where he is a finalist in Superstar II, he sings his nearly classical Arab songs with a melodramatic and beautiful voice. Despite his laughter, his eyes retain a serious demeanor. Surrounded by glitz, fashionable show presenters, and a fervently screaming teenage audience, he seems out of place. When asked by a jury member why he is so reserved, he replies that he cannot sing joyfully when his people in Palestine are facing so many difficulties. He mentions the people dying at checkpoints. For him, art is a form of resistance, and he adds, "Art is a

bird." It can carry messages across borders. Alongside the Libyan contestant Ayman, Ammar takes center stage in the final of the popular competition.

Large screens have been erected in many public spaces across the West Bank. After the show, cars cruise the streets slowly, honking, and people chant rhythmically, "Ammar, Ammar!" "Imagine," says Mary's cousin, "it's like *mamnou'a tajaawel* [curfew] when he sings. You can hear his voice echoing through the streets, much like how people in the West watch a major football match on TV."

Anyone can vote, whether through email, fax, or SMS. There is an overwhelming surge of support for Ammar in numerous countries, including the Gulf States, where he works as a waiter. And undoubtedly, also in Palestine. In the past week, people have been casting their votes on a massive scale. The local telephone company announced a special discount for voting calls, and computers were set up in various locations for the public to use. I've heard that someone voted six times, each time using a different name. Others had multiple email accounts, which they used to cast multiple votes. Palestinian families advised their relatives and friends abroad to fulfill their duty. It's a national mobilization effort, lasting until Sunday when the votes are tallied and the final result is revealed.

Indeed, Ammar emerged as the winner.

Certain political factions expressed dissatisfaction with the public's interest in Ammar and Western-imported TV shows in general, leading to the closure of outdoor displays. This sentiment was not uncommon during both the first and second Intifadas, when celebration parties were often prevented or disrupted due to concerns about insensitivity to people's ongoing suffering.

A few years later, summer 2013, another victory unfolded.

At midnight, we ventured out onto the streets of Bethlehem to join a spontaneous celebration. A motorcyclist raced forward for about hundred meters along the usually serene University Road, arms triumphantly stretched out in the air. A car sped over a small hill, briefly hanging in the air before touching down. Bethlehem erupted in jubilation for Mohammed Assaf, a twenty-three-year-old from the Khan Younis refugee camp in Gaza, who had just secured victory in Arab Idols. This level of spontaneous joy was unprecedented in Bethlehem. Cars adorned with Palestinian flags filled the streets, people leaned out of windows or perched on car roofs, horns blared, brakes screeched, and engines roared. Amidst the cacophony, a woman leaned out of a car window and exclaimed, "*mabrouk sha'ab al-falastin!*"—congratulations, Palestinian people. We responded in kind, shouting back our congratulations.

Social media buzzed with activity, with Jara energetically participating. The TV competition, broadcast across the Arab world and viewed globally, required viewers to determine the winner through text messages sent to Lebanon. Palestinian telephone companies distributed free phone cards to facilitate sending numerous messages. Some companies offered messages as a bonus for purchasing their products, even a cup of coffee. While the Egyptian competitor could potentially rely on millions of votes from Egyptians, Assaf, a handsome man with an impressive voice, ultimately garnered around 65 million votes.

Just the previous day, we featured him in a workshop for religious studies teachers as an example of the moral principle of "giving." The discussion revolved around whether Mohammed had given a gift to the Palestinian people or if he was more of a recipient, receiving status, money, and a lavish car. The consensus was that he had certainly given, and generously so. Mohammed provided a sense of national unity through his songs, such as "Up, the *kufiyeh*!" In his performances he intentionally mentioned various segments of the Palestinian people that needed acknowledgment, including prisoners and the fallen. One after another, he acknowledged the different geopolitical "sections" of the Palestinian people—those fragmented involuntarily: Palestinians in Gaza and the West Bank, '48 Palestinians (residing within Israel), Jerusalemites, Palestinians in Lebanon, Jordan, Syria, and Palestinians in the diaspora.

Mahmoud Darwish, the Palestinian poet, once stated that while people around the world live in a homeland, Palestinians are unique in that the homeland lives within them. It's a sentiment that resides in their hearts and distinguishes them as a special community.

Mohammed is a religious individual, but not a fanatic one. The imam of Nablus in the West Bank, who issued a *fatwa* against the glitzy show, did not find widespread support for his stance. Rumors circulated that the Palestinian Authority attempted to recruit Mohammed against Hamas, but the Gaza-based wedding singer declined to participate in this political maneuvering.

It's a form of cultural resistance. Mary conveyed a text message to her friend that morning: "Good morning, victory." Her friend's reply was: "Good morning, dignity." In response to a skeptical observer from Qatar who failed to comprehend the exuberance, a Palestinian stated, "Let us savor victory for just one day." After all, the show hadn't altered the underlying situation.

⸎

On November 2, 2017, Ya'acoub Shaheen, a Palestinian Christian from Bethlehem, also participated in the new Arab Idols competition. He garnered popularity, especially within Bethlehem, and was among the remaining candidates along with Palestinian Amir, who resided in the US.

One of the jury members, Ahlaam, a Saudi singer, directed critical and even harsh comments towards Ya'acoub at one point, much to the dismay of the audience. The following day, Facebook brimmed with mockery and photoshopped images of Ahlaam, who is actually quite affluent, evident from her sparkling jewelry. During a staged interaction in the show's dressing room, Ya'acoub gifted her a Quran adorned with mother-of-pearl from Bethlehem.

Telecommunication companies facilitated voting for Palestinian candidates through SMS. Moreover, several buses journeyed from Bethlehem to Amman and then by plane to Beirut. Residents of Bethlehem eagerly traveled to see Ya'acoub perform live and support him in the finals, while also relishing a few days of holiday and perhaps visiting the sanctuary of Mar Sharbel, a renowned saint from the Lebanese mountains known for his healing abilities.

During a celebration at Tamer's Frères (de la Salle) School that week, Ya'acoub's name was mentioned, and he was applauded as a former student of the school. Similarly, Mary Atrash, also from the same school, was acknowledged for her recent participation as a swimmer representing Palestine in the Rio Olympics.

In reality, people are yearning to hear and share stories of success and achievement, even if largely symbolic, particularly within a general atmosphere where it's common to assert that the situation has never been worse.

The Birthplace of Jesus Is in Palestine

In March 2017, Ya'acoub Shaheen received a warm and enthusiastic welcome in both Bethlehem and Ramallah. Following his victorious performance on Arab Idols in Beirut, he didn't just greet VIPs; he also visited and performed in several Palestinian refugee camps near Beirut alongside his fellow contestant Amir Dandan who is originally from the town Majd al-Krum in the Galilee. The residents of these camps always yearn to see individuals coming from Palestine. And just like the previous week, there was yet another vibrant street celebration in Bethlehem, complete with Syriac-Orthodox and Palestinian flags waving proudly, with Ya'acoub being hoisted on shoulders. This festive moment provided a respite from the usually disheartening news of the time. (In February alone, 420 Palestinians were detained by the Israeli occupation, according to *Maan* News Agency in Bethlehem.)

Tall banners adorned with Ya'acoub's image were draped along apartment buildings, a testament to the outpouring of support. The local business community rallied behind him, with numerous companies covering the cost of the SMS votes, which amounted to 3,5 shekels each (almost one Euro). It seems that many millions of votes were cast for him. Votes came from both Christian and Muslim communities in Palestine, including places like Hebron where he studied, as well as from Arab communities around the world and across the Arab region.

Remarkably, where Palestinian politics often struggles to unite its people, Ya'acoub achieved a sense of unity. At Arab Idols, he gave voice to a spectrum of identities. His performances transitioned seamlessly from Syriac-Orthodox songs to Palestinian anthems (including the well-known schlager *"ween 'a ramallah,"* or "where in Ramallah"), and even to a newly composed Arab song addressing the toll of "damned wars," sung alongside fellow contestants.

Equally significant is Ya'acoub's genuine likability among those who know him personally. He actively participates in charity concerts without seeking payment. Addressing the crowd at Nativity Square, he emphasized that money and fame would not change him; he would forever remain a "son of Bethlehem."

His triumph instilled a palpable sense of dignity and presence among Palestinian Christians. Recently, Mary encountered an elderly Palestinian Christian man on the street who engaged her in conversation. He had constructed a substantial house in Bethlehem with the intention of passing it down to his five children. However, he lamented that despite raising them to live here, they eventually left for the US, and he feared they might have to sell the house.

Mary deeply empathized with his sentiment. Presence, or sumud, entails more than just physical location; it's also about forging connections with others who share a common background and an unspoken sense of dignity and pride in their heritage. These feelings among Palestinian Christians were revitalized by Ya'acoub, at least for a fleeting moment.

⸎

Another widely recognized competition that garnered attention in Palestine was the World Cup 2022. Alongside the Moroccan team, who made it to the semi-finals, the Palestinian or Palestine identity emerged as winners, at least among the Arab crowds. The sight of numerous Palestinian flags being consistently waved both on the field and among the audience members was a prominent and heartening display.

Furthermore, the Arab mother took center stage. The Moroccan players and coach took turns dancing with their mothers on the pitch, an act that celebrated their often unsung heroines. The familial sumud, the steadfastness within their families, played a crucial role in propelling the players to achieve their pinnacles.

The victories in the music competitions and the accomplishments of the Moroccan national soccer team, along with their vocal support for Palestine, have stood as much-needed little victories for Palestinian sumud.

The performances of Palestinian singers on television platforms serve as a representation of Palestinian cultural identity. They also forge connections among different segments of the Palestinian population, uniting them with one another and with the broader Arab world, if only for the moment. But it's important to acknowledge that while these performances have been dynamic cultural moments, their participation from viewers has been limited, often confined to voting and celebrating.

9

Challenging the Wall

THE PERIOD WHEN THE Rachel's Tomb area served as the welcoming gateway to Bethlehem's northern side seems like a distant memory.[1] Prior to 1993, when a checkpoint between Bethlehem and Jerusalem was set up, the central thoroughfare of the area, the Hebron Road, was only a short car ride away from Jerusalem. Along this road, Rachel's Tomb stood as a modest structure that didn't attract much attention from pilgrims of the three monotheistic religions.

Following the June War in 1967, the Hebron Road exhibited stately houses, shops and restaurants in a relaxed ambiance. The commercial district was frequented by Israeli Jews and Palestinians alike due to its close proximity to Jerusalem and the comparatively affordable prices. Refugee families from the nearby 'Aida camp have memories of picnicking around Rachel's Tomb in those times.

In the course of the Oslo years in the 1990s and the second Intifada that began in 2000, two military walls were erected around Rachel's Tomb. First, a relatively small wall was constructed, which was later circumvented by an eight- to nine-meter high Separation Wall. In 2002, after effective lobbying by religious-Zionist settlers, the tomb was de facto annexed to Israel. Walls and roads linked the complex to the main military checkpoint between Bethlehem and Jerusalem.

During the second Intifada, Rachel's Tomb underwent a transformation into the dystopian architectural structure it remains today. It became a

---

1. See for a more in-depth account of the Rachel's Tomb area, Van Teeffelen, "Rachel's Tomb," 56–59.

Challenging the Wall

symbol of exclusion, control, and surveillance, characterized by an intricate system of cameras, watchtowers, and walls.

Access to the holy site was restricted solely to Jewish and international pilgrims, while local Christians and Muslims were barred. Iron gates sealed off entry to the Tomb. With the fragmentation of the Hebron Road and the relocation of the checkpoint to a narrower entry road, the area around Rachel's Tomb lost its vibrancy. During the second Intifada, most shops along the main road were forced to close. Many local residents avoided the area due to the continuous presence of the Israeli army, which conducted home searches and detained people for interrogation or imprisonment. Inhabitants often had to sleep on the floor. Tourist buses exited the area as quickly as possible, tourists looking out of bus windows at the towering walls, often oblivious to their impact on the local population.

The Rachel's Tomb military structure is part of the separation Wall in the West Bank constructed by Israel mainly in the 2000s. Approximately 712 kilometers (or 442 miles) long upon completion, the Wall consists of a combination of barriers and obstacles designed to prevent movement of people between Israel and the West Bank.

As expected, the fortress at Rachel's Tomb attracts Palestinian youth and children, particularly from the neighboring 'Azza and 'Aida refugee camps. Engaged in a dangerous game of cat-and-mouse, the youth throw stones while soldiers respond with tear gas, rubber bullets, and sometimes worse.

At the Arab Educational Institute, located near the Wall, we have been thinking how to express sumud by challenging the Wall at Rachel's Tomb. We knew about the many creative activities on or near the walls in separated cities such as Berlin and Belfast in the past. I myself have a background as a member of solidarity and peace movements in Holland, and so am particularly interested.

One notable form of cultural resistance is the use of graffiti. While some parts of the Wall remain untouched, other sections have become canvases for layers of paint that carry messages of opposition, hope, and solidarity. I remember from the early times the graffiti: "I want my ball back"; "I don't need no walls around me! —Pink Floyd," and "Another world is not possible—she's on the way. Many of us will be here to greet her, but on a quiet day, you listen very carefully, you can almost hear her breathing —Arundhati Roy."

The Birthplace of Jesus Is in Palestine

Some graffiti take on a non-political discourse that focuses on human freedom and the longing for connection. The imagery of walking over, flying over, or looking through the Wall signifies a desire to transcend physical barriers and reassert the universal human right to move freely and connect with others. This type of graffiti reflects a shared aspiration for a world beyond the confinement imposed by the Wall.

In July 2006, shortly after the construction of the Wall in Bethlehem, I conduct an interview with Abdalla Abu Rahmeh, who speaks about the anti-Wall actions in the village of Bil'in west of Ramallah:

> Our actions are intended to expose the injustice of the Wall and the treatment of Palestinians. Last week, we wore orange masks similar to those worn by convicted individuals before their execution. It was meant to reveal to the world what is occurring in Gaza. When you destroy power stations, you are taking lives. Last Friday, we staged a soccer play of sorts, with adults carrying a large ball on their shoulders while wearing T-shirts and carrying flags representing different countries participating in the World Cup. On the opposite side of the field, twenty children wore red-painted T-shirts symbolizing the occupation. The message: While everyone watches football on TV, many Palestinian children are losing their lives. With each action, we introduced a new element. We encased ourselves in barrels, boxes, jails, cylinders, and cages. We taped our mouths shut, chained our hands, and chained ourselves to the Wall.[2]

In 2008, I accompany Jara home after she attends a cartoon animation workshop at the institute. Ten children, all around Jara's age, collaborated to create a story. The narrative was brought to life through illustrations. Characters were cut out and shaped into Chinese silhouettes, which were then digitally animated.

Jara is beaming with pride about her contribution that morning. "Papa," she exclaims, "the story is about a girl who always enjoys *mlukhieh* [a spinach delicacy] at her grandma's house. She visits every week. Once,

---

2. Interview Abdalla Abu Rahmeh by author, Bethlehem, July 2006.

grandma gave her a dress with a rose on it. That's why she's named Warde, which means "flower." She's like a Palestinian Red Riding Hood. But suddenly, there's this towering Wall. You know the one, daddy, that tall one over there. Now, Warde can't go to grandma's anymore. So, she and her friends brainstorm about what they can do. First, they try throwing something that explodes, but that doesn't work. The Wall doesn't budge. Then they attempt using a ladder, but when they reach the top, there's no ladder on the other side, and they can't jump.

"Then," Jara's eyes twinkle with excitement, "a sort of wizard appears. He has the power to bring anything drawn on the Wall to life. Warde decides to draw a bird. The bird magically comes off the Wall, and Warde sits on it, flying over the Wall. Over the next few days, she creates different drawings that help her overcome the Wall. Pretty neat, huh, daddy?"

Afterwards Jara eagerly explains to Tamer how to create cartoons, make images move, and bring a bird to life.

2009: During the last few years, AEI has developed what came to be called the Sumud Story House near the Wall at Rachel's Tomb, as a meeting point for women's groups and later on youth groups. At this new House, I discuss the upcoming Sumud Festival near Rachel's Tomb with Rania, the leader of the house. She conducted a study among the inhabitants of the area about their lives and cultural resistance. The festival theme is freedom. Rania's children are musically gifted. She herself serves on the board of the local Edward Said Conservatory. Her three young children are slated to perform together on a rooftop overseeing the Wall. Rania embodies determination and sumud, raising her children single-handedly as a working woman with the support of her extended family after her young husband's passing.

Music can be a powerful expression of freedom. For the festival, we encourage attendees to bring pots, pans, and spoons. Around fifteen scouts from St Joseph School join us with their large drums, which they typically reserve for the Christmas procession. I enthusiastically remark how wonderful those heavy drums sound. However, an invited school choir opts out due to concerns from the school management about the location's proximity to the Wall. We feel they need to be a bit more courageous, even though we can't predict if the Israeli army might intervene. Though our event is right in the heart of Bethlehem, it is in zone C, like all the streets bordering the Wall. The Israeli army holds control.

Antoinette, a spirited member of AEI's women's group despite her advanced age, will be playing her accordion. She also brings along children from her extended family who are accustomed to performing a few Christian or nationalist songs when foreign groups visit.

The Bethlehem Sumud Choir, comprising over 20 women from the Institute, sing national songs, folk songs, and tunes that celebrate Muslim-Christian living together. They often perform for international visiting groups, shedding light on daily life in Bethlehem and conveying what freedom means to them.

FIGURE 5

Bethlehem Sumud Choir in front of the Wall

As for suitable freedom symbols, we decide on keys, a symbol that holds musical significance as well. Everyone present, dozens of people, form a large living key, and Rania organizes an exhibition of drawings by the women's group in the shape of a key. In 'Aida camp, an enormous key has since many years been displayed above the camp's entrance, representing the key to the homes from which the refugees were displaced—in essence, a symbol of the right to return. This is a departure from the typical symbols like pigeons, balloons, or kites often used during actions against the Wall.

⌁

Soon, on December 11, 2009, an important document known as the "Kairos Palestine" document will be released by a comprehensive and representative group of Palestinian Christians. This document indirectly supports the Boycott, Divestment, and Sanctions (BDS) campaign as an alternative to perpetuating cycles of violence. Prolonged peace negotiations have failed to end the occupation, instead masking a harsh reality. The document advocates for nonviolent resistance as a means of preserving humanity and even as a way of saving Israelis from themselves.

⌁

2011: The "Wall Museum"[3] takes form, displayed on large, weather-resistant story posters made from thin metal fixed to the Wall. Just yesterday, we placed the first twenty-four posters where the Wall surrounds the Rachel's Tomb shrine. Initially we had put story posters on the interior walls of the Sumud Story House, then decided that we could also put the posters on that larger Wall outside.

The first poster introduces the Museum as an initiative by the House, aiming to convey the real-life stories of Palestinian women including the members of the women's groups which convene at the House. "These stories highlight suffering, oppression, as well as sumud—the inner strength and cultural identity that we choose to reveal about Palestinian life, which the Wall attempts to conceal and suppress." Each story is accompanied by a vertical line of heritage embroidery, intentionally positioned without forming a frame around the story to avoid the stories being "imprisoned."

However, the practical aspect of putting up the posters proves to be no simple task. Workers stand on ladders, carefully attaching the large, thin-metal posters using iron nails. Meanwhile, two military watchtowers loom above us, and four Ecumenical Accompaniers from the World Council of

---

3. See for more details and examples of stories, Murra, "The Wall Museum," and Arab-Educational Institute-Pax Christi, "Resource: Wall Poster Stories."

Churches are present, supporting our safety. A few journalists arrive to document the event.

Mary has requested that her own story be placed in a prominent location. Her story recounts her reaction when nine-year-old Jara was ordered to undress in public at a checkpoint. Another tale involves Ein Karem, the birthplace of St John the Baptist, and the site where the Virgin Mary met her cousin Elisabeth. A Palestinian woman from the village writes about her family's expulsion in 1948 and their subsequent prohibition from visiting their former home.

As I read the Ein Karem story, it inadvertently brings to mind the Magnificat, the hymn of the Virgin Mary which is displayed in a courtyard of a church in Ein Karem which we sometimes visit. The hymn commemorates Mary's meeting with her cousin Elisabeth and contains lines that accuse the powerful, expressing sentiments of "casting down the mighty from their thrones and lifting up the lowly" (Luke 1: 52). This connects with the messages shared by Palestinian women in their stories. In later years, the women's choir would create a video featuring songs about "the birth of Jesus between the Walls," including a modern-style Magnificat.

Passing by are vans selling gas cylinders, their squeaky announcements reminiscent of the sound of military jeep loudspeakers. To lighten the atmosphere, we share jokes. A colleague quips that the army should consider upgrading one section of the Wall due to the cement's subpar quality for holding the iron pins. We jest about having the most well-protected museum and suggest visitors could leave evaluation forms in the small horizontal opening of the adjacent military watchtower—the symbolic throne of the powerful.

Upon completing our modest project, we admire the twenty-five posters with satisfaction. They resemble pages in an open testimonial book, with the added advantage that they can be photographed and shared more widely. We eagerly anticipate how they will fare during the upcoming Christmas days.

꩜

2016: We expand the Wall Museum towards a desolate area near 'Aida refugee camp, situated on the western side of Rachel's Tomb.

Challenging the Wall

Oral histories play a pivotal role in unveiling and documenting personal stories of the past, capturing the nuances of human experience. Nevertheless, oral history interviews typically reach only a limited audience of scholars and students. The Wall Museum serves as a platform to present these oral histories to a broader, non-academic audience.

Although each of the 110 stories is not as exhaustive as a traditional oral history account, their impact stems from their presentation in a readable format for passersby. This specific approach to sharing oral history is a form of community resistance. The collective narratives highlight a shared humanity and dignity that stand in stark contrast to the dehumanizing effects of the Wall.

Numerous posters convey the events of the Nakba in 1948, during which 700,000 to 800,000 Palestinians were forced to leave their homeland. Last week, Palestinian communities commemorated the Nakba. In one instance, old trucks that were used during that time were brought back into service, forming a procession.

One of the new posters features a reflection by Mirna al 'Azza from Beit Jibrin camp. She recounts how she accompanied her elderly grandmother to the ruins of Beit Jibrin, her grandmother's place of origin from which she was forced to flee in 1948. Mirna writes, "I walked behind her, climbing up a hill in the village. She seemed much stronger and capable of walking faster than I remembered. She knew exactly where we were going, as if she had been there yesterday."

Certain Wall posters showcase contemporary reactions of youth from 'Aida camp to photographs of fleeing refugees and devastated villages from 1948. One particular photo depicts a refugee woman in shock and despair, holding a cloth before her mouth. A boy remarks that this image reminds him of women in the camp today who cover their mouths to protect against tear gas.

Further along, on a street renamed "End of the World Rd," small posters display quotes from Palestinian poet Mahmoud Darwish. These quotes engage with the desolate surroundings, such as "The last train has stopped at the last platform and no one was there," or "A mother reprimands the prison guard: 'Why have you spilled our coffee onto the grass, you mischief maker?'" "A human being is a bird unable to fly."

Within this dystopian landscape, the youth, staff, and volunteers at AEI gather for cleaning tasks. With the support of Bethlehem municipality staff and equipment, we clear piles of garbage near Antoinette's house. Antoinette, the former music teacher in 'Aida camp, conducted music lessons for children in her family's cellar during the shelling of the Second Intifada, providing comfort. Her story is also featured among the Wall posters.

Among the rubbish, we collect numerous tear gas and other canisters found near the gate. To those who still reside in the area, we explain our cleanup efforts as a means to explore the potential for music and sports activities. Some skeptically inquire, "So you come here for a few hours and then leave?"

At the end of 2016, the Wall Museum is composed of 170 large thin-metal posters, showcasing personal stories of Palestinian youth and women. It occasionally attracts unexpected visitors.

※

In 2017 Israeli soldiers arrived at the museum site and proceeded to read approximately fifty stories aloud at two o'clock in the morning. One soldier read the stories in English through a loudspeaker while another soldier provided Hebrew translations. The entire event was recorded on a tape recorder, almost resembling a military operation.

Claire, a member of AEI's women's group residing in a house surrounded by Walls and poster stories, experienced sleeplessness for several hours that night. The repeated mention of "Sumud Story House," a signature at the end of each of the stories, echoed in her ears.

I imagine how intriguing it would have been to witness the soldiers reading the story of Mary and daughter Jara.

The sudden interest from the army in reading the stories raises questions. Perhaps it was curiosity or a desire to assess whether the stories could be seen as a form of "incitement." The fact that the stories are being read by foreign visitors and Palestinian guides in the area may have drawn the army's attention. Despite Mary's belief that the army didn't pay much attention to the stories, the incident where soldiers tore down an "Apartheid Rd" street sign associated with the Wall Museum hinted at a different reaction.

FIGURE 6

Wall story poster

The Walled-Off Hotel is located across from one of the Walls around Rachel's Tomb. It opened in 2017. The play on words with the luxurious Waldorf Hotel chain, combined with its creative and thought-provoking interior decor, makes for a unique and impactful artistic statement. The hotel is a canvas for artistic expression and political commentary, engaging visitors in a thought-provoking dialogue about the situation on the ground.

We are the hotel with "the worst view in the world," advertises the Hotel. It has been decorated and furnished by London graffiti artist Banksy. Inside, you feel as if in a colonial-style British afternoon tea party. Looking closely you can detect the irony in the images and objects. A collection of Israeli observation cameras shoots out from the wall like pistols, placed above a series of carefully selected Intifada catapults, and below a series of royal China plates.

A well-kept museum of political history inside is introduced by a tableau of the moment when, hundred years ago, British Foreign Secretary Arthur Balfour signed his declaration that promised Palestine to the Zionist movement as long as the rights of the "non-Jewish" population, then ninety percent of the total population, were not harmed. In the background is a window with a view on the Thames and Big Ben next to a map of the British Empire.

Since the streets and houses along the Wall are located in Area C, under direct Israeli military control, it is in principle possible for Israelis to enter the hotel. The hotel actually invites them to do so. But that too is not without irony, because Israelis have to travel through Area A of the Palestinian Authority to get to the hotel, which Israeli law does not allow. They are also not allowed to pass the nearby Israeli checkpoint. In practice, Israelis will continue to travel only on the other side of the Wall, visiting Rachel's Tomb, which is inaccessible to residents of Bethlehem though it is in the midst of their city. Once Jara looked through a crack in the Wall into the other side, straight into the eyes of a surprised Orthodox Jewish girl at the Tomb.

Years ago, Banksy made stencil graffitis on the Wall in the middle of the night, including images of girls frisking a soldier or floating over the Wall hanging on a balloon.

Opposite the hotel entrance used to be a Wall poster telling the story of a girl, Christie, who lived nearby. "As a teenager I went through a lot. I saw a man being shot right in front of my eyes and I saw an Israeli shooting at our house. Yet I never stopped laughing and hoping."

Banksy's arts brand stands for a range of oppositional narratives; perhaps mostly the decolonizing movement for Palestinian rights.

The hotel-café has become a convenient starting and end point for explorers of the area. Near it is a place to buy paint for those interested to make statements on the Wall in front. Several small shops nearby sell Banksy's graffiti on posters and other souvenirs, and others copy Banksy or, like the anonymous "Cakes Stencils" artist, bring their own graffiti themes of children living and playing in an absurd and violent world.

The concept of "existence is resistance" resonates with people facing various forms of oppression and injustice around the world. The stories of individuals and families who continue to live their lives despite the obstacles they face highlight the indomitable human spirit rooted in the connection to the land, culture, and community. It refuses to be erased.

The various ways in which sumud is expressed, from oppositional counter-spaces through arts and cultural activities, to checkpoint economies and businesses adapting to new circumstances, demonstrate the resilience of people in the face of exclusion and dehumanization.

In 'Aida camp, the cultural resistance against the confined and militarized environment takes the form of national symbols, names of prisoners and martyrs, historical references, and community empowerment initiatives. By displaying symbols of identity and resistance, the residents of the camp assert their presence and agency.

The Noor Women's Empowerment Group's initiative in the camp to share meals and teach Palestinian cooking to foreigners not only promotes cultural exchange but also contributes to the education of disabled children, showing how cultural activities can have a positive impact on both the community and the individuals involved.

The Wall itself becomes a versatile backdrop for various cultural expressions. It can function as a stage for performances, a canvas for artwork, a setting for stories, photos and films, and even a makeshift screen for projections. This adaptability allows for a wide range of creative small forms of resistance that capture the attention of passersby.

10

Hiking the Land

THE VILLAGE OF BATTIR, to the southwest of Bethlehem, sits at the border of the invisible Green Line that separates the West Bank from Israel proper. Adorned with Roman-era terraces, pools, small water channels, and archaeological sites, it offers spectacular views of idyllic agricultural fields and valleys, as well as an old railroad and even a small, abandoned station operative in the British mandate time. It reminds me and others in the Bethlehem area of how life can be abundant in a hilly, open environment graced by real horizons, in short, as Mary would say, where you can "breathe." A place to distract ourselves, to escape the open air prison of Bethlehem. In the course of time it became an area where my family and I used to go out regularly for walks and a leisurely sit at one of the restaurants. As a concept expressing love for the earth, sumud is obviously related to the ecological need to protect the earth and let it blossom.

In spring 2001, I ask Sana'a, the independently-minded local head teacher, why the inhabitants of Battir have still not established a folklore center to celebrate its great landscape. It seems difficult to get the families to cooperate.

This week the Nakba or disaster of 1948 is commemorated. Across the West Bank, Gaza, and among Palestinians in Israel, demonstrations and parades are held.

I visit the annual school festivity, well-organized by the indomitable Sana'a. To avoid criticism for hosting a joyful *hafle* [party] during a time of mourning for the dead and wounded, she instructs teachers and students to keep all songs, dances, and attire in the national style, emphasizing Palestinian identity and solidarity. The hundreds of mothers present visibly enjoy the atmosphere. For years, I have observed that young girls from Battir have a talent for folklore dance and drama. They truly feel free in their movements.

One play depicts a Palestinian young man discontented with his impoverished life in Palestine: "I am eating only bread and olives, olives and bread." Against his mother's wishes, he leaves the country and marries a foreign woman. In an attempt to forget his Palestinian ties, he withholds the fact that his mother is still alive from his wife. However, his wife expresses a desire to see the village from which he originated. Upon arrival, his mother recognizes him and wishes to embrace him, but he avoids her. The story unrelentingly portrays that he cannot escape his destiny: Israeli bullets critically injure him. When his mother is willing to donate her kidney and blood to save his life, he reconciles with her. He invites her to join him in the West, but his wife tells him, "No, we are going to stay here." And so it unfolds. Throughout the play, Israeli military airplanes intermittently break the sound barrier, their presence both distant and immediate.

When teacher Suzy conducted an oral history project with her eleventh graders at St Joseph, a girl from Battir, Amal, recorded an interview with her grandfather, covering protests during the British mandate period.

HISTORY OF BATTIR: SOLIDARITY AND FIGHTING SPIRIT

> After the end of the First World War, Turkey left Palestine and Britain took its place. Britain acquired or confiscated land from Palestinians for Jewish settlement. This led to the eruption of Palestinian anger in the 1936 revolution.
>
> The rebels had two main demands: the annulment of the declaration about a Jewish homeland in Palestine and a halt to the purchase or confiscation of Palestinian land. However, these demands were rejected. The people and rebels grew even more furious. Their first action was to punish Palestinians who sold land to Britain. In our village [Battir], a few individuals sold land to Britain, and those people were imprisoned or even killed by the rebels. On a particular night, many village men gathered in the town square when a group of rebels suddenly appeared, inquiring about specific people. They took those individuals and subjected them to severe beatings. No one dared to defend them, as they

would have suffered the same fate. As they were considered traitors to Palestine, I believe they deserved it.

The rebels' second action was to sever any communication with Britain by blocking roads and railways that connected the village with other regions. Village residents supported the rebels and stood by them. They offered shelter, security, assistance, and food. The women played a significant role. They cooked for the rebels every day. One woman would keep watch on the road, ready to alert the villagers when soldiers approached. She would signal with a secret phrase to indicate imminent danger: "It's cloudy, it's cloudy, everybody!" Upon hearing this, the villagers would swiftly hide the food and put out the fire, acting as if nothing had happened. If they were caught cooking a large amount of food, the soldiers would realize it was for the rebels and discard it.

The British High Commissioner was aware of the rebels' actions, including the disruption of communication between Palestine and Britain. (. . .) The following morning, British soldiers flooded the village, arresting all adult men from Battir, Al-Khader, Hussan, and other nearby villages. The men were confined to a square without food, but their families secretly sent them food. This occurred frequently. Several times, people were pursued by planes and targeted with machine gun fire. People were killed just as they are today.

There was a positive aspect to our lives. We lived in harmony, united as one. We would rise early and head to the fields. Your grandmother would bake that delectable bread and bring it to us in the fields. It was simple but incredibly delicious. We spent the entire day working, returning home exhausted. Yet our fatigue was physical, not emotional. This indicates our happiness. When we laughed, it came from the depths of our hearts, unlike today. Many times, we would stay over at my brother's house, staying up late into the night, chatting and laughing until we drifted off to sleep with smiles on our faces.

During the harvest season, we would assist one another, working until the last person finished their field. Life would have been unbearable if we hadn't done that. My daughter, nowadays I sleep on a comfortable bed, I no longer work, and I enjoy the finest food, but let me tell you, I do not sleep through the night.[1]

---

1. Owaineh, Amal, "I Was Born In War. I Have Lived In War. And I Feel That I Will Die In War." In: Atallah, *Your Stories*, 10–14.

Hiking the Land

Back to March 2001. A teacher speaks to a group of the Institute's youth about the history of education in Battir, highlighting the number of academics the village has produced, and expressing frustration over the current state of education. Following this, we discuss non-violent actions to draw attention to the constrained way of life. We gaze at the stunning terraced fields bordered by a settler road.

I propose the bird as a symbol of education. Birds can carry one's spirit to distant horizons. "Speak, bird, speak again," family members used to exclaim during long winter nights when they wanted their mother or uncle to continue recounting folk stories. Social scientists Muhawi and Kanaana wrote a folklore book with that title.[2] According to some, Battir means "house of bird."

Students agree and add more natural elements to the bird: air, seeds, flowers, sun—"that's all we need." We brainstorm the advocacy effects of kites and balloons, noise and prayers, as ways to convey the message of freedom.

It would be wonderful, I believe, to be able to do something akin to the paintings of Chagall—to soar through the air, above houses and hills. Like in a dream. Once, a girl from Arroub refugee camp near Hebron described her visions of peace as her body flying across the Jordan River. She dreamed of studying there and then returning to help her people. Even I myself, holding a foreign passport, share such flying dreams. They should resonate with many here.

The connection to the land and the yearning for freedom used to find expression in the practices of the summer harvest, which were characteristic of the region. My Arabic teacher, Aida, spoke at length about it. Her family owns land in the Maghrour valley, situated in the countryside west of Beit Jala, between Beit Jala and Battir. The following account is from July 2008.

> Fifty to sixty years ago, the residents of Bethlehem, Beit Jala, Beit Sahour, and even Jerusalem would venture into the countryside for extended picnics. The majority of townspeople participated. For example, everyone in Beit Jala would go to the Maghrour. The Maghrour is a highly fertile area suitable for agriculture. All the people in Beit Jala owned or rented land in the countryside.

---

2. Muhawi, *Speak, Bird*.

The *nuzha* wasn't a single-day picnic. It spanned several months. People would arrive in April or May and stay, with intermittent breaks, in the countryside until September—from Easter to the Feast of the Cross on September 14. Some even stayed until October, when the olive harvest occurred and required substantial labor. However, during that season, they returned home in the evenings due to colder October weather.

I remember it vividly, even though I was a small child at that time [Aida was around seventy years old when she recounted this]. People went to the countryside to tend to their fruits and vegetables. The countryside was open, offering space and fresh air. It felt like an extended picnic. If folks had work in town during the day, they'd head to the countryside in the afternoon. Sometimes, ten members of an extended family would go, while around forty remained behind. The following week, another ten would go. Similar practices existed in Lebanon and Egypt.

It took about half an hour to reach the countryside by foot or on a donkey. Cars were nonexistent. People brought easily portable food, small items of furniture, compact kitchen utensils, and burners for cooking simple fare, as there were no refrigerators, of course. When they harvested many vegetables or fruits, women carried them back to town in a large basket on their heads. Then they'd return to the countryside.

Every day involved cooking. They used the produce from fruit trees, like grapes and apricots, and vegetables like tomatoes. Wells were available for drinking water. Coffee or tea was brewed, and fresh bread was baked in the low stone oven, known as a *tabboun*. Meat and other foods were barbecued, releasing a delightful aroma. They cooked various foods, such as pigeon or chicken, on a burner and placed it on flatbread from the oven. They supplemented their meals with olives and olive oil, figs, dried figs, or tomatoes. It was sufficient. They enjoyed simple fare like salads and lentils. People preserved foods for winter, like dried tomatoes, grape raisins, and dried figs.

Everyone was content. Friendships flourished, laughter echoed, and people enjoyed each other's company. Children played games. Some would put their young children or a baby on a homemade swing under a tree. Television and electricity were absent. About ten families stayed in the same field as neighbors. They visited and mingled with each other. In the evenings, all the men gathered together. They sang popular songs, often quite lengthy, and danced while clapping. I recall they used a gramophone powered by batteries, housed in a box with a sizable loudspeaker.

Storytellers recounted tales of individuals named Abu 'Issa and Abu Hannah, and stories from ancient times, folk narratives. Most people were illiterate, so they memorized the stories. When someone spoke, children would commit the tales to memory. After a year or two, these stories were passed on to others. Remember, fifty to sixty years ago, few attended school. These stories were drawn from the rich history of Arab literature; they were real accounts. Someone would stand up and commence telling a story, or they would invite someone to share: *"ya flaam..."* [oh people...]. Men told these stories.

Women narrated tales for the younger ones, the children, like those about the *ghouleh* [witch], or stories involving animals. These stories were recounted earlier in the evening. I recall there were elder men who recited poems, sometimes accompanied by a *rababeh* [a type of violin with a single string]. These poems were memorized too. They were akin to stories.

People stayed awake after dinner, from around eight until midnight. Everyone did so. They slept in the small "castles" constructed from stones and rocks. Beds and mattresses were brought along. There might have been caves where they slept, or they rested on rooftops or under large trees. They even crafted little huts from tree branches, akin to the Jewish Sukkoth festival.

It was a simple and joyful life. Visitors and family members came from Jerusalem and Jaffa, relishing their time in Beit Jala. All of them shared in the food, the singing; they were united. They conversed, listened, all together, regardless of whether they hailed from the vicinity, Jerusalem, or Beit Jala. They exchanged the latest family updates. People held each other in high regard. Life was nearly devoid of conflicts. If someone needed to bring fruits to town, they handed it to another person to carry, or they borrowed donkeys from one another. In Beit Jala and Bethlehem, homes were left unlocked; there were no thieves. Doors were left slightly ajar. The houses didn't contain anything valuable. People had mattresses, beds, cupboards; nobody sought to possess anything expensive at home. Life was affordable in those times.

Weddings were not held in the countryside; they occurred in town, at homes. The church, the priest, were necessary. Such festivities spanned several days. They took place before summer, in the spring. During summer, people were preoccupied in the countryside. Today, it's different: all weddings are during summer.

Two years ago, following the forty years during which my family owned the land near Everest [the summit of Beit Jala], the Wall was planned there. The twelve dunams [1 dunam = 1000 square meters] were expropriated. Now, going there is a concern, it's prohibited. About three to four years ago, we went to collect olives there, but that's no longer possible.³

Over the years, Battir has gained renown for its hiking opportunities. Sana'a dedicated herself to promoting hikes among her teachers and at the Institute. Her school had the finest view of Battir's terraces and the railway. In the confined Palestinian setting, hiking offers a means to connect with the environment, even if it entails taking longer routes to bypass checkpoints or other obstacles. However, many schools are apprehensive about organizing hikes due to student safety concerns.

While Mary attends the festivities at Bethlehem University, which is celebrating its fortieth anniversary, Tamer (now eleven years old, it's 2013) and I set off on our hike to Battir. Tamer agrees to join the hike with the condition that he can bring his iPad. The trip by service or shared taxi is economical: eleven shekels or just over two Euros for two people. We commence near the Hassan Mustafa Center, one of several cultural centers recently established in Battir. Recently, I had the opportunity to meet Nadia Butma, who manages the center named after a former community leader, Hassan Mustafa, who safeguarded the village in 1948 and negotiated the precise ceasefire line with the Israelis.

Battir has been contending against the construction of the Wall for several years. If built close to the village, the Wall would not only disrupt the lives of the local people but also significantly harm the landscape—the stunning terraces adorned with trees, wells, caves, as well as ancient Roman channels, pools, and tombs. Strolling through the area gives you a sense of timelessness, especially when encountering a farmer with a donkey tending to the land.

3. Interview Aida Kattan by author, Bethlehem, July 2008.

Hiking the Land

FIGURE 7

Battir landscape

Tamer and I huddle together to keep warm; the weather is chillier than expected. I explain to him the concept of *sinsile*, the charming small walls that adorn the terraces, constructed from the rough stones found in the surroundings.

The feeling of timelessness shatters when Tamer notices two military jeeps on a road near the Har Gilo settlement, and the Wall becomes visible in the distance—lower than in Bethlehem, as the settlers wish to preserve the views from their homes.

❧

Mary is currently (2018) occupied with food. She is coordinating a cooking course for teenagers at Bethlehem University. Jara is one of the participants and tests her new skills at the family dining table. The teenagers partake in an excursion to learn about traditional agriculture and the environment. Each Palestinian village or town is known for a particular fruit or vegetable and celebrates it with its own agricultural festival. This time, they take a stroll in Battir, renowned for its aubergines.

The youth perspire profusely after a 1,5 hour walk with breaks. Mary cheers them on: "Look at those old houses; they are much more captivating than the modern ones." The recently established Landscape Eco Museum, with an aubergine as its logo, has issued a map of the area. Hikers can follow designated trails. Scarcely any readily available maps of the Bethlehem surroundings exist, whether for villages or desert regions.

Traditionally, people are accustomed to relying on memory instead of maps. Moreover, many new maps are extraordinarily intricate, displaying elements like the Wall, the Green Line (the invisible border between the West Bank and Israel), settlement areas, and more. Few places in the world necessitate such sophisticated and colorful geopolitical maps as the West Bank does. At least now, a few guides with trails and local maps are accessible.

―

Battir boasts a growing number of restaurants with breathtaking vistas.

A few weeks ago, my colleagues at work and partners congregated at a restaurant in the Maghrour area. The Qassieh family owns land there equivalent to a soccer field, about half a hectare. They manage a well-known restaurant called the Maghrour restaurant. This area falls under Area C, the portion of West Bank lands under complete Israeli civilian and military control.

The restaurant is situated a bit far away, and Mary and I hadn't visited it before. However, the Institute provided an opportunity on the occasion of the departure of a German volunteer sent by Pax Christi Stuttgart and Aachen, who had been with us for a year. The early evening meal tastes delicious, and the surroundings are delightful, surrounded by abundant green trees and bushes, far from the noise and traffic of Bethlehem.

As the dinner concludes, we feel rejuvenated and make a promise to ourselves to return, with or without a hike.

The Qassieh family exemplifies sumud by holding onto their land. Like many others, they have been caught in Kafkaesque Israeli High Court proceedings that have lasted for years, if not decades. Despite this, they have persisted, even though several structures on their land have been demolished. In area C, many lands are not officially or historically registered, although they are well-known to belong to specific Palestinian families. Adding to this, almost no Palestinians receive building permits in area C from the Israeli army/Civil Administration. Over sixty percent of the West Bank is classified as Area C, and it is currently the focus of upcoming colonization and annexation efforts. For someone like me who is interested in the nuances of language, it's striking to observe how the constant talk about Area A, B, C, or even Z (as a restaurant in Ramallah humorously names itself) renders Palestinian lands nameless and anonymous. Linguistically, it becomes a blank canvas, ready to be claimed.

In 2018 the Jewish National Fund, the primary landowner in Israel, suddenly presented evidence of land ownership that nobody knew. Supposedly, the family land was sold nearly fifty years ago. In a statement regarding the case, the Israeli peace organization Peace Now refers to the Jewish National Fund as the "Fund for the expulsion of Palestinians."[4] The Israeli High Court did not allow any further appeals from the family. The main house was demolished, streamed live on Facebook for Bethlehem residents and others to witness.

In recent years, house demolitions have escalated at an exponential rate in the West Bank and East Jerusalem. In 2018, around seventy apartments or houses were demolished in the village of Sur Bahir to the east of Bethlehem. These structures were not in area C, but in area A and B, under Palestinian civil control, and built with permits. The rationale for these demolitions was that the houses were situated within a 250-meter area on both sides of the Wall designated by the army as a "security" zone.

As is the case throughout the West Bank countryside, the presence and influence of settlers are growing, including in Battir and the Maghrour.

It is 2020. I am enjoying a pleasant hike in the company of my family and guests, walking from Battir through the Maghrour to Beit Jala, where we currently reside. Along the way to Beit Jala, we unexpectedly encounter some young adults walking, wearing *kippahs* [Jewish head coverings]. They seem quite at ease, and while they might be carrying weapons, it's not visible.

Mary directs my attention to the private lands of the mayor of Beit Jala, located nearby the valley. Beyond the hilltop lies the spot where the Maghrour restaurant was dismantled last year, taken over by the Jewish National Fund. Somehow, the presence of the young settlers who walk freely through these areas seems to convey the message that they not only assert their claim to the land but also feel entitled to appropriate it. Nearby

---

4. Peace Now, "KKL-JNF is fighting," and also Peace Now, "KKL-JNF and its Role."

The Birthplace of Jesus Is in Palestine

settlements reinforce this sentiment, and I suspect there are Israeli surveillance cameras scattered amidst the beautiful olive groves. After our trip concludes, Mary reads a Facebook post from another hiker in Beit Jala who encountered "settler shepherds" along the same *wadi*.

The Institute collaborates with a school in Battir, where a group of fifty teenage students have chosen an advocacy activity aimed at promoting the continued development of domestic and international Palestinian tourism in Battir, capitalizing on the beautiful hiking paths available.

The school, situated along the famous railroad and also in Area C, is closely monitored by Israeli cameras and occasionally visited by Israeli security personnel.

The students believe that the project helps them grow as individuals and develop a deeper appreciation for the surrounding Palestinian lands and orchards. Naturally, the issue of litter left by picnickers is a concern. However, what's of greater significance to the students is the encroachment of settlements and settlers' activities, which render the hiking paths unsafe for Palestinians—developments such as the construction of new settler roads, the presence of settlers in proximity to Palestinian hiking areas, and the promotion of religious and archaeological sites for settler tourism. The land is filled with both actual and claimed graves of individuals considered holy in Jewish, Muslim, and Christian traditions, or sites associated with various religious events.

In Walajeh, a village near Battir with a complex history of displacement and resettlement, and faced with numerous house demolitions, the villagers are accustomed to visiting a traditional picnic spot near the spring of 'Ein Haniyyeh. Presently, the spring ('ein = spring) attracts both Jews and Palestinians. The complex encompasses two pools, surrounded by archaeological remnants, and situated within a vast expanse of approximately 120 hectares, primarily owned by the villagers of Walajeh. Historically, it was frequented by villagers and, many years ago, by Christian, Muslim, and Jewish pilgrims who attributed special healing properties to its water. The terraced lands, a testament to the dedication of generations of Walajeh's farmers and those from neighboring villages like Battir, have been meticulously preserved for hundreds, if not thousands, of years. However, it seems likely that Palestinians will eventually be prohibited from visiting the site, let alone participating in its development for domestic tourism. Once again, settlers and settlements play a pivotal role in excluding local Palestinians from their own landscapes.

Hiking the Land

In late summer 2021, during yet another hike around Battir, we set out for 'Ein Haniyyeh. The weather is splendid, basking in the warmth of late summer.

Years ago, we visited this spring with friends, witnessing firsthand how the Wall physically separated the villagers of Walajeh from the spring and the encompassing terraced lands. It left the farmers of Walajeh forced to sneak onto their own private lands, harvesting fruits as though they were acting as thieves in the night. Today, we are taken aback by a new development. 'Ein Haniyyeh and its surrounding lands have been transformed into an Israeli park. Access is still possible for villagers, albeit via a detour, since the entrance to the park is located on the West Bank side of the checkpoint leading to Jerusalem. Like others, they are now required to pay an entrance fee.

The visitor demographics comprise mostly Jewish Israelis, alongside a few Palestinians. Some individuals swim in the larger pool. In contrast to the past, the site now exudes an air of meticulous order. Everywhere, there are fences, railings, clearly demarcated pathways, directional signs, and cautionary notices.

The interpretive signs suggest that we stand on a site of Jewish heritage known as Nahal Refaim National Park, with names like Judea and Mount Gilo prominently featured, accompanied by a quote from the Book of Isaiah. The archaeological remnants predominantly date back to Roman times, and among them is an early Byzantine church currently under the ownership of the Armenian Patriarchate. According to Christian religious folklore, 'Ein Haniyyeh is the site where the apostle Philip baptized an Ethiopian Eunuch on their journey to Gaza, an event detailed in the Book of Acts (8:26-29).

Mary and I take in the refreshing air and absorb the surroundings with a sense of contentment.

The uncertainty lies in whether Palestinians from the West Bank will be allowed to visit this site in the future. Israeli plans entail moving the checkpoint several hundred meters into the West Bank, ensuring that park entry is exclusively accessible from the Israeli side and not from Walajeh or other West Bank locales. Although the Jerusalem municipality is spearheading the checkpoint's relocation, lengthy legal proceedings—in which international law is hardly a consideration—are impeding the process.

The Birthplace of Jesus Is in Palestine

Why this deliberate "slowing down"? It's worth pondering; after all, the Israeli authorities can expedite matters if they choose. My impression is that many of these more "contentious" annexation endeavors, including those involving lands near the Cremisan Monastery near Beit Jala, are intentionally protracted. Not solely to give the transformation the veneer of a complex planning initiative, but also to allow Palestinians and the international community to gradually come to terms with these new facts on the ground. A swift takeover would more blatantly resemble the robbery that is indeed transpiring.

Moreover, the meticulous attention paid to local archaeology suggests that Israel's actions are serving a broader civilizational purpose, implying that their presence is firmly embedded in this area.

A representative from Ir Amin, an Israeli organization advocating for a shared Jerusalem between Israelis and Palestinians, points out the overt intention of the Israeli authorities in their actions: "The Israeli authorities aren't even hiding the fact that the site is for Israeli residents only, whereas the farmers who built and preserved the terraces—which are the pretext for building the park there—are being removed from the area."[5] The representative further states, "The park also creates continuity between Jerusalem and the Etzion Bloc [of Jewish settlements south of Bethlehem], turning al-Walaja into an enclave, isolated and threatened" (as quoted in *Haaretz*, 16/3/2018).

In and around Bethlehem, as well as other Palestinian cities, settlers increasingly embark on journeys to historical and archaeological sites, such as the Solomon Pools to the south of Bethlehem near the village of Artas and the terraces of Battir to the west. While these journeys may appear tourist-oriented, they carry a more deliberate message. Quite recently, Israeli Prime Minister Bennett encouraged Jewish Israelis to visit springs, parks, and archaeological sites in the West Bank, possibly in an attempt to desensitize local Palestinians to the ongoing appropriation.

The Institute, over the past years, has collaborated with various school communities around Bethlehem, actively advocating for the preservation of Palestinian heritage at these springs and archaeological locations for the local population. One of the lessons learned is the importance of Palestinians continuing to visit these sites, despite the apprehension of encountering armed settlers.

---

5. Berger, "Israel Pushing Plan."

Hiking the Land

Leaving 'Ein Haniyyeh, we cross the road and venture into the forest path leading to Battir. There are no signs to guide us, and we quickly find ourselves on the wrong road. A Palestinian swimmer in the 'Ein Haniyyeh pool directs us onto the correct path. Palestinian workers in Jerusalem and Israel are well-acquainted with these concealed routes, often used to bypass the Jerusalem checkpoint. Later, we spot Israeli helicopters scouting the area for what they label as "illegal" Palestinian workers.

The path becomes clearer, and we arrive in Battir with joyful anticipation of purchasing its renowned aubergines. We savor fresh lemon and orange juice at a restaurant, gazing out over the terraced landscape. As Mary often remarks, it's a bittersweet experience to feel content and at ease while remaining acutely aware of the harsh realities.

It is autumn 2020. Settler activities take on particular prominence during the olive harvest season. Gathering olives is not just a task but also a celebratory tradition. It has historically involved the collective effort of neighbors and friends. Upon completion, people would congregate, sharing food and camaraderie. The olive groves hold profound significance for Palestinians, representing an extension of their concept of home that extends across the hills, offering breathtaking and expansive vistas. Sadly, these vistas are gradually diminishing or being obstructed.

Mohammed Khatib, a notable figure known for years of protests by landowners against the construction of the Wall in Bil'in near Ramallah, has shifted his role to become a spokesperson for the new organization *Faza'a*. The term *Faza'a* translates to a call for help during war in Arabic. This organization mobilizes Palestinian volunteers to safeguard landowners during the olive-picking season. Khatib suggests that the increased incidents involving settler youths may be attributed to their boredom stemming from the COVID-19 pandemic.

Khatib notes, as reported by *Haaretz*[6], that larger groups of settlers are entering olive groves this year, often causing damage and engaging in attacks while the Israeli army observes. With each passing year, the territory designated for Palestinian harvest is reduced, while settlements continue to expand. This situation has resulted in violent clashes during harvest time. Khatib emphasizes the gravity of these incidents, stating that if one seeks a

6. Hass, "Palestinian Volunteers."

significant indication of the impact of occupation, it lies in what transpires in the olive groves.

These acts of violence against Palestinian farmers contribute to a broader pattern of dispossessing Palestinians from their lands. According to a report in *Informed Comment*[7], Palestinians plant around 10,000 new olive trees in the West Bank each year. Shockingly, Israeli settlers have destroyed approximately four thousand trees so far this year. The combination of feeling unsafe during harvest and witnessing their crops being destroyed discourages Palestinians, particularly the youth, from maintaining a strong connection with the land—a vital component of sumud.

According to *Haaretz*[8], thousands of Palestinian families own lands situated beyond the Wall and require permission to access them. There are forty-six seasonal gates in the Wall or fence that open only a few times throughout the year, while twenty-eight gates open either daily or three times a week. This limited entry to olive groves, which I've observed in the situation in north Bethlehem, where Mary's family can only access their land for picking a few times annually, is a scenario that robs the experience of joy during the harvest. Ultimately, it's designed to facilitate the gradual takeover of the land by nearby settlements.

---

7. Samaana, "Israelis Destroyed."
8. Hass, "Palestinian Volunteers."

11

Reclaiming Beauty

WHILE TRAVELING TO THE village of Artas south of Bethlehem in 2001, I engage in a conversation with a taxi driver, a Bethlehem University graduate. The driver reveals that he now earns more as a taxi driver than he did working as a psychologist in the local mental hospital. With fluent English and a business diploma from the United States, he emphasizes the pervasive potential of making money through hard work, even in the Palestinian territories. The driver's words leave me unsure of how to respond.

Upon arriving in Artas, I notice posters on the walls depicting a Fatah figure who was recently killed by the Israeli army. The taxi driver confirms that the person in the posters is his cousin. The village residents had gathered at the mosque that morning to mark the end of the forty-day mourning period. The driver expresses a desire to leave the country for a few years, particularly to the US, to raise awareness about the Palestinian situation among people from different backgrounds. He anticipates that the Israeli lobby would prevent him from continuing to live if he pursued such efforts. Despite his business-like demeanor, the driver's sense of despair is palpable.

Artas, the village we are visiting, is situated on a hillside and home to approximately five thousand Muslim Palestinians. The village is characterized by numerous caves that hold coins and artifacts dating back to Roman and Canaanite times. The area holds significant archaeological value, and the presence of five natural wells contributes to the lush green surroundings. Last year, I guided groups of tourists to witness women washing clothes in the village well, highlighting the ongoing traditional practices.

However, the romantic imagery contrasts with the village's present water scarcity, although it is relatively less severe than in neighboring areas.

Close to Artas are the Solomon Pools, three large water reservoirs, two of which were built during Roman times to supply Jerusalem with drinking water. Over time, the pools also served Artas, but the water quality declined. They became known as a recreational picnic spot and a dangerous swimming location where several young people have drowned over the years. Plans for the future involve utilizing the pools for tourism purposes, yet ongoing development projects have halted due to the second Intifada. A nearly finished four-star hotel opposite the pools suffered damage from shelling.

Musa Sanad emerges as a significant figure for his dedicated efforts in developing a heritage center and folklore museum in Artas village. His initiative led to its inclusion in the Bethlehem 2000 project. His inspiration dates back to the 1960s and 1970s when he delved into the numerous anthropological and folklore studies centered on Artas, conducted by foreign academics, missionaries, and adventurers. These scholars were drawn to the village's hospitable environment, pleasant climate, lush surroundings, and its proximity to Bethlehem and Jerusalem. One prominent researcher was the Finnish anthropologist Hilma Granqvist (1891–1972), who conducted several renowned anthropological studies in Artas. As an anthropologist myself, Artas always inspired me as a source of folk and other stories during my stay in Bethlehem.

Hilma Granqvist, affectionately known as "*sitt* [lady] Halima," spent about three years in Artas during the late 1920s to early 1930s. Initially focusing on research about women in the Old Testament, she shifted her focus to the unique culture of Artas after recognizing its distinct characteristics. She meticulously documented various aspects of domestic life, including childbirth, child-rearing practices, circumcision, weddings, divorce, and funerary customs. Granqvist's approach involved in-depth, long-term studies of a specific village community, setting a precedent that other mostly female researchers and photographers of the village later followed.

Granqvist's practice, familiar among anthropologists, of not declaring the name of the community she studied initially concealed her connection to Artas. Even today, some of her works remain unavailable at Bethlehem

University. Mary took an effort to gather Granqvist's out-of-print books, which are essential resources for those interested in Palestinian culture. Recently, Granqvist's extensive studies and photographs have been made publicly available through a dedicated platform.[1]

In the mid-1990s the project "Removing the Classroom," conducted during my time with the Ramallah-based educational NGO Al-Mawrid, one of the educational narratives highlighted Palestinian school students in Artas engaging in role-play, reenacting the first encounter between local village women and *sitt* Halima.

In Artas, *sitt* Halima resided in the home of Louise Baldensperger, the daughter of a missionary from Alsace, who had lived in the village for many years. The book *From Cedar to Hyssop*, a delightful exploration of Palestinian plant folklore written by Grace Crowfoot with Louise Baldensperger as the main informant, stands as one of the most charming works about historical Palestine.

Drawing parallels with biblical narratives, traditional Palestinian peasant life drew wisdom from connecting the human experience with the surrounding flora and fauna. Nature served as a prism through which the body, relationships, and human qualities were given meaning. For instance, the bride is often compared to a pomegranate for her beauty.[2]

In the context of peasant society, plants were often attributed symbolic characteristics that reflected their role in people's lives. For instance, the saying "The vine is a town lady, the olive an Arab and the fig a peasant woman"[3] is explained in this manner by Crowfoot and Baldensperger: the delicate vine requires care like a town lady, the olive can grow on the mountains and protect itself like an Arab, and the fig tree, essential to peasants, is homely and typically planted near villages.

Back to 2001. Accompanied by Musa and Jamal, a local teacher and landowner, I visit a plot of land called Khirbet al-Khookh [ruin of the plum]. The intention is to explore the potential of purchasing or renting the land for the development of a school garden where students from various schools could participate in agricultural activities and environmental care. Other

---

1. https://granqvist.sls.fi/#/home.
2. Crowfoot, *From Cedar to Hyssop*, 111.
3. Crowfoot, *From Cedar to Hyssop*, 27.

concepts involve creating a religious garden with plants mentioned in the Bible and the Quran, as well as a human rights project where students could visit nearby sites. However, we come across an Israeli tank stationed nearby, a stark reminder of the ongoing conflict and occupation.

Musa playfully suggests that the land's beauty might have been an inspiration for Solomon to write the Song of Songs. I acknowledge the wealth of stories that the land holds, which can serve educational purposes. The notion of turning dreams into reality is discussed, including the potential of constructing a small restaurant, a dream of Musa's.

Being an anthropologist, my interest lies in old customs and rituals that were once shared by Muslims and Christians in Palestine. For instance, on May 5th, both Christian and Muslim families visit the nearby village of Al-Khader to pray for prosperity in the local church of St George. This cultural practice exemplifies the traditional connection Palestinians have with the land.

Just across a small, picturesque green valley in Artas, nestled beneath a hill, stands a 125-year-old elegant church and monastery named the Closed Garden, or Hortus Conclusus. The very name Artas is related to the Latin *hortus*, meaning garden. The church is owned by an Italian order of nuns who commemorate the valley as the "enclosed garden" and "sealed-off spring," echoing passages from the Song of Songs (4:12). The term "enclosed garden" carries echoes of the forbidden Garden of Eden or Paradise. I feel a connection to the church, partly because Mary's ancestors were involved in its architectural design. Nearby, there are remnants of the ancient town of Etam, a fortified city from over 2500 years ago during the era of the southern kingdom of Judea.

RECLAIMING BEAUTY

FIGURE 8

The Hortus Conclusus Church in Artas

The Biblical Song of Songs carries particular significance for Artas. Palestinian poet Mahmoud Darwish, a national figure who passed away in 2008, frequently referenced the Song of Songs in his work, viewing it as a love lyric representing the convergence of various Mediterranean and Asian civilizations.

In an interview book titled "Palestine as Metaphor,"[4] he discussed how his poetry was influenced by the Song of Songs, and explained that the poetry of the Song of Songs is a result of the convergence of civilizations, namely the Sumerians, Egyptians, and Canaanites.

Darwish regarded himself as influenced by various cultures and cultural works, including the Bible. He mentioned that if he were to write his own Book of Genesis, he would structure it as a dialogue among the successive cultures of Palestine. Holy texts belong to all of humanity, and the eastern Mediterranean is the birthplace and nurturing ground of great human civilizations.

In the early 20th century, a Palestinian priest from Beit Jala named Stephan Stephan, part of a group of missionaries and adventurers visiting

---

4. Darwish, Mahmoud. *Palestine as Metaphor.* See for an account of the Biblical influences on Darwish' work: Raheb, "Biblical Narrative."

the area, collected proverbs and wedding trills from Palestine. He meticulously analyzed the Song of Songs, referencing these local proverbs and folklore. According to his perspective, the proverbs and trills he found shared both content and form with the Song of Songs. Here is a summary of Stephan's comparison between the lover in Biblical and contemporary Palestinian love poetry, as articulated by the historian and anthropologist Salim Tamari:

> His love for her inspires him to describe her with a variety of pretty appellatives, common to both periods [biblical and Palestinian], such as dove, reed, an enclosed garden, a spring shut up, a fountain sealed; a garden fountain, a well of living water. He is captured by her beauty; first he considers her fair, and then as spotless (. . .) to him she is at the same time a rose in a flower garden, and a proud horse. (. . .) [H]er breasts, seemingly the most attractive part of her graceful person, are to the old singer like wine, even far better. We consider them as pomegranates and rarely as clusters of grapes.[5]

According to a theologian I met years ago, who extensively studied the Song of Songs (I prefer to keep her anonymous), the predecessors of the rabbis and the church fathers seemed to have felt a degree of discomfort with the book due to its evident erotic nature. Even before its inclusion in the canon, the Song of Songs was allegorically interpreted. In this interpretation, the woman symbolized the people of Israel, the man represented God, and their actions represented God's historical relationship with His people. The tradition of allegorical interpretation continued with the church fathers, who saw the song as a depiction of the love between God/Christ and the church. The Virgin Mary also played a role in this interpretation, with the enclosed garden sometimes being associated with Mary's virginity.

However, this approach underwent a shift during the Enlightenment. Since then, the Song of Songs has been primarily seen as a love song, and the allegorical interpretation took a back seat. From that point onwards to the present day, several intriguing discoveries have emerged, including links to Egyptian and Assyrian love poetry (*wasf*), women's perspectives, and the Song of Songs as a form of drama.

---

5. Tamari, "Lepers," para 26. Tamari cautions against a "nativist" interpretation of present-day proverbs resembling the Songs. For the original article, see: Stephan, "Palestinian Parallels," 199–278.

Contemporary readings of the Song are open and influenced by new theological approaches. It's possible to interpret the song as a sequence of parodies, ironies, pieces of drama, or a patchwork of various songs and poems associated with Arab weddings. Traditionally, people would intertwine such songs and stories during activities like harvesting, with the beloved becoming synonymous with the landscape and vice versa. The bodily gifts would blend with the gifts of nature.

If there's a central theme to the Song, it could be the strength of love, a notion that perhaps parallels the concept of sumud. For instance, Song of Songs (8:6) reads: "Set me as a seal upon your heart, as a seal upon your arm; for love is strong as death, passion fierce as the grave."

My Arabic teacher, the late Aida, once shared that in the *hammam*, the public bath—such as the former Hammam Miriam near Lion's Gate in the Old City of Jerusalem where she once resided—it was customary for the bride to display her beauty to the loud cheers of attending women from different religions and ethnicities, forming a chorus of celebration.

As mentioned, numerous anthropologists have delved into daily life in Artas, resulting in over ten monographs about the village over the years. Could these insights be used for a theological re-evaluation of the Song of Songs alongside a fresh tourism initiative that showcases Palestinian village life, its bountiful offerings, and its traditional, affectionate beauty—some of which resonates with the Song?

Returning to the reality of present-day Artas, there's a sense of reclaiming some of the beauty also associated with sumud.

We move to the corona year 2021.

"The COVID-19 crisis is one of the most impactful experiences of my life. I felt a responsibility to support the people in my village,"[6] says Faten from Artas. A twenty-nine-year-old mother of one, she works as a kindergarten teacher and volunteers at my Institute in Bethlehem.

Artas is Faten's hometown, facing challenges similar to other Palestinian communities in the West Bank: farmers' lands are occasionally

---

6. The quotes of Faten are taken from her notes written down in the context of an AEI-Pax Christi project coordinated by the British aid organization CAFOD and supported by the European Union Peace Initiative (EUPI) and CAFOD, "Engaging, empowering and equipping diverse and marginalised youth and amplifying their voices for peace," 2000.

inaccessible due to restrictions imposed by the Israeli army; the neighboring Israeli settlement, Efrata, encroaches upon village territory; and the Wall stands tall in the surrounding hills.

Young women in Artas undergo training that equips them to recognize community peace challenges, devise solutions, and effectively communicate them to decision-makers. Faten actively participated in this campaign.

She ardently supports the Institute's sumud advocacy approach, which she believes has transformed not only her life but also the lives of other young women in the village. To Faten, sumud encapsulates the endeavor to keep the community connected to the land, unite people for collective welfare, care for the vulnerable, and uphold the values of mutual respect and environmental stewardship. Sumud signifies not only service and sacrifice, but also the joy of embracing beauty and a profound sense of belonging to a dignified shared home.

"Artas deserves to shine as the most beautiful," she asserts. "While I was at university, my sole ambition was to graduate and secure a job. However, after engaging in this project, my perspective shifted drastically. A sense of responsibility grew within me, and my sense of belonging deepened."

The women embarked on a lobbying effort within their local council and went door-to-door, urging residents to fulfill their waste collection tax obligations. Consequently, new bins were stationed along the streets, and garbage collections became a daily routine. Collaboratively, the young women and their families painted old car tires, adorning them with flowers and placing them along the roadsides. They raised awareness about waste issues in schools and the broader community.

"We encountered numerous challenges, whether stemming from patriarchal traditions that preferred women to remain at home or from broader societal norms. This campaign not only altered the village landscape, but it also transformed perceptions of what young women can achieve. Most importantly, it transformed me. I have evolved into an ambitious woman seeking a better future."

This resilience and solidarity have been particularly evident over the past few months. Despite the additional burdens brought about by the pandemic, mutual support has surged. Nearly 30 young women initiated various efforts to assist vulnerable members of their community. They raised awareness, prepared meals for families in quarantine, and offered practical, medical, and psychological aid.

"Throughout the crisis, we rediscovered ourselves, uniting as one community."

Across the spectrum of local initiatives undertaken by young women's groups over the past couple of years, the concept of "cleansing" society—enhancing the community's beauty, serenity, and love as a shared abode—remains at the heart of their efforts. These young women stress the importance of enhancing the village's aesthetics as a means to capture the world's attention and garner support for their rights. Faten shares this concern wholeheartedly.

"At times, I feel a mixture of sadness and fear. The fear stems from the encroachment of the Israeli settlement onto our agricultural lands. What will become of us and our children? We also grapple with apprehensions about Israeli proposals to annex portions of Palestinian territory. Ultimately, my hope is that this pandemic will conclude, granting everyone good health and security. My dream is to live in a state of peace, in this land of tranquility, free from fear."

12

A Resilient Presence

IN MANY CASES, it is a characteristic of Palestinian sumud to transform the home and the land into a site of opposition, while also inviting and engaging others in defending them.

A notable example is the nonviolent movement in the village of Bil'in, west of Ramallah, which among many other actions placed playground equipment in front of bulldozers and soldiers. The action aimed to illustrate how the construction of the Wall threatened the fabric of daily life. Caravans were positioned on land facing potential confiscation or exclusion. The home and its surroundings were relocated to the "frontline" as a form of challenge.

A home and the environment that defines or encircles it, can thus be strategically recreated as part of a struggle against land expropriation and Wall construction. This approach connects with the universal resonance of the concept of home, familiar to all.

It is February 2012. Heavy rain falls. The bus driver greets the passengers with *"Sabah al-Ward"* [morning of the flower] as they shield themselves under their raincoats. The greeting carries a hint of sarcasm, but not overly so, as rain tends here to uplift people's spirits. Rain sustains the land and nurtures the plants.

On this January morning, I accompany a Dutch group visiting the Tent of Nations. Located on a hilltop near the sizable village of Nahalin,

A Resilient Presence

south of Bethlehem en route to Hebron, it is an ecological initiative by a Palestinian family that resolutely clings to their land despite various pressures. The army has created a hill of rubbles in order to block the entry road so visitors need to climb a little to arrive at the farm, on a low hilltop surrounded by other hilltops populated with settlements. Daoud Nassar, the spokesperson, welcomes us into a spacious cave since the army prevents him from constructing on his own land. A farmer and a gentle yet strong speaker and storyteller, he embodies the spirit of the project.

As its name implies, the Tent of Nations serves as a meeting point, for both locals and internationals. Its mission involves creating educational and ecological projects for Palestinian children and youth. Hospitality and care become tools of resistance. Amidst the uncertainty they face, the family plants olive trees that yield fruit only after several years, symbolizing their steadfast faith in the land and its people amidst external pressures.

What's truly noteworthy is that their endeavors unfold amid a prolonged siege and uncertainty. Despite the presence of settlers from nearby settlements who damage trees and create an intimidating atmosphere, the Nassar family engages in a legal battle that spans decades. This struggle involves extensive efforts, including lawyer visits to Istanbul (to investigate land deeds from Turkish times) and London (from the British Mandate era). Despite the substantial legal expenses, the family's determination remains unshaken. This is not merely a fight for survival, but a principled display that underscores the ultimate triumph of humanity and spirit—a liberation struggle embodied in the daily actions of a family.

Daoud juxtaposes this resistance with three alternative options: embracing blind violence and hate, resigning oneself to occupation, or opting for emigration. In line with nonviolent philosophy, he asserts that he refuses to perceive Israelis as enemies, even in the face of their persistent attempts to dispossess his family and their land.

It is May 2016. "Please, come forward!" The Nassar family is called onto the stage to introduce themselves. Present are the mother, brothers, sisters, and children. Each family member briefly shares their deep attachment to the land before an empathetic audience of around hundred, comprising both young and older individuals, including many international participants and former volunteers.

Despite the continuous difficulties the family confronts—ongoing court battles, demolition orders, and destruction of fruit trees—they remain steadfast, upholding a legacy of struggle that spans multiple generations. The legacy reaches back a century, to when the land was initially purchased. The meticulously preserved land deeds serve as vital documentation for their legal fights.

Their struggle encompasses a mother who courageously cared for 10 children single-handedly, and who presently cooks for visiting groups, as well as a grandfather who marked his daily labor with evening prayers within the cave that he and his successors called home. Daoud Nassar recounts that as far back as 1936, during the Arab general strike, the family confronted the destruction of 25,000 fruit trees.

Established in 2002, the Tent of Nations initiative represents a commitment to not surrendering hope, maintaining a presence, refusing violence, and upholding hospitality. It is scripture translated into action.

The current festival culminates a three-day series of workshops, encompassing explanations of Bible stories, mosaic crafting, folk dancing, and advocacy for justice. The performances encompass a diverse range of local and international groups. A Brass for Peace ensemble contributes a festive atmosphere, featuring four younger Nassar family members. The German country music group *Without Borders* plays familiar songs like "Take Me Home, Country Roads" and "Blowin' in the Wind."

For me, the highlight is the *dabkeh*, the traditional Palestinian folk dance. Jihan Nassar, Daoud's wife and a computer teacher who also works in the nearby town of Nahalin, proudly introduces the international participants whom she taught the basic *dabkeh* steps in just three days. Then the experienced Beit Sahour *dabkeh* group takes the stage, consisting of six young men and women who exude confidence as they perform. *Dabkeh*, as Jihan explains, is tied to the moment feet touch the ground, a rhythmic touch that resounds audibly. Once the group syncs with the music and rhythm, their faces light up and their bodies emanate self-assuredness. They follow the music with a jumping rhythm that reminds me of horseback riding, a sensation of freedom unencumbered by obstacles.

Among the various group leaders and country representatives, Meta from the Netherlands receives extra applause for her months of dedicated work to organize the festival. She reflects on what resonates most deeply about Palestine and the Tent of Nations: the convergence of two extremes, the extreme vulnerability that people face and the remarkable inner strength they display.

A Resilient Presence

As the backdrop to the festival, the settlement of Neve Daniel rests on the neighboring hill. I hear that a group of settlers has been observing the festivities, perhaps surprised or curious? Another world, yet so close.

Following the performances, we engage in discussions about the prevailing situation. Several visitors observe the worsening conditions in "Area C," the dry bureaucratic term that underscores the land's fragmentation. The Tent of Nations itself lies within Area C. Slowly but persistently, Palestinian villages and Bedouin communities in this region face a form of ethnic cleansing.

Palestinian poet Mahmoud Darwish once expressed, "The Palestinians are the only nation in the world that feels with certainty that today is better than what the days ahead will hold. Tomorrow always heralds a worse situation."[1] However, he also noted, "Palestinian people are in love with life."[2]

Sumud embodies a resilient presence. Even amidst mounting pressures, the Tent of Nations perseveres. In 2021, the family faced physical attacks from neighboring villagers who sought to claim parts of their land.

In a single year before corona struck, 2019, the family hosted no less than 13,000 people who visited the Tent of Nations and heard its story. The website: "We hope that those people from over 40 countries who came to see, went back home motivated and told the Tent of Nation's story of hope, faith and love."[3]

Another narrative of a resilient presence unfolds in a campaign to preserve access to the Cremisan Monastery.

To the west of Bethlehem, certain lands are threatened with becoming inaccessible, such as those near the Salesian Cremisan Monastery and the village of al-Walajeh. On a particular Friday in 2011, I join attendees of the Kairos Palestine conference to stand on this land as a form of resisting presence. (Kairos Palestine promotes a document formulated by Christian

---

1. See https://www.brainyquote.com/quotes/mahmoud_darwish_526850#:~:text=Mahmoud%20Darwish%20Quotes&text=The%20Palestinians%20are%20the%20only%20nation%20in%20the%20world%20that,always%20heralds%20a%20worse%20situation.

2. https://www.brainyquote.com/quotes/mahmoud_darwish_526852

3. https://tentofnations.com/

Palestinians two years ago, calling for nonviolent resistance against occupation, deemed a "sin").

Under the olive trees, Father Ibrahim Shomali leads a mass. I reflect that to pray here is to exist, to be present before witnesses, and that such existence itself constitutes resistance. Participants share the potency of connecting with the land—standing upon its rocks, observing delicate flowers persevering even in winter.

A speaker mentions how residents of Beit Jala still recall their childhood ability to view areas as distant as the outskirts of Amman to the east and the Mediterranean to the west from this spot. My Arabic teacher once vividly described the people of Bethlehem and Beit Jala, who would leave their homes during summer, spending weeks on their lands to harvest fruits in the western regions of Beit Jala. They'd tell stories in the evenings and slumber under or within trees, beneath the stars.

We partake in a sacramental presence. Bread is shared, followed by the Palestinian peasant breakfast of thyme, bread, and olive oil. A Palestinian woman from the Galilee remarks on Israel's quiet appropriation of Palestinian cuisine, like falafel, labeling it as Israeli. Rooted deeply yet exposed and vulnerable, the human Palestinian presence stands in stark contrast to the fortified presence of settlements.

We recite the Our Father prayer in numerous languages. Laughter and handshakes offer some solace. While escaping the rain, a colleague in the car tells me that locals observe the actions of activists and NGOs but see little in terms of tangible outcomes. A pervasive discomfort persists due to the lack of an end in sight to land expropriation.

That morning, *Haaretz* reports that the Efrat settlement will expand further north, encroaching upon Bethlehem's southern villages, particularly Artas. Bethlehem is now encircled by settlements to the north, west, and south, while the east, near the desert, remains undeveloped.

Concluding the Kairos Palestine conference in the field, former patriarch Michel Sabbah shares an unconventional prayer of the Franciscans, stating that we must pray to feel discomfort about our surroundings; we must pray for anger, as anger is what we require.

※

"We Are Not Absent" read the button distributed during another public outdoor mass in the fields near the Cremisan Monastery. The Monastery is located in a verdant, beautiful area and known for its winery, a wine festival, and extensive olive groves. The olives from Beit Jala are considered one of the best in the area. Many people are used to go there to visit one of the very last forests in the Bethlehem area. Like Battir, Cremisan is a cherished picnic spot for Bethlehem residents.

It's Friday, June 1, 2012, marking the culmination of the annual World Week for Peace in Palestine and Israel, convened by the World Council of Churches. The choice of the enigmatic phrase "We Are Not Absent" by the organizers holds deliberate significance.

Recently, seven thousand dunams or seven hundred hectares of land between Jerusalem and Bethlehem, owned by 182 landowners from the Bethlehem area, were designated by Israel as "absentee property." Why? Mainly because these Christian landowners were denied access to their land for years, except for a few days annually. The term "absentee property" seems emblematic of the colonization of Palestine, once dubbed "a land without a people for a people without a land."

Nevertheless, the people persist, active and engaged, including at Cremisan. Former Jerusalem patriarch, Mgr. Michel Sabbah, once again leads the Mass beneath the silver-gray olive branches and upon the rocks. He emphasizes that the moral and physical presence of Palestinians and Palestinian Christians cannot be erased. The Holy Land should be a place of security, justice, and peace for both peoples. Drawing on the New Testament episode depicting Jesus overturning the moneylenders' tables in the Temple, Mgr. Sabbah declares that the Holy Land has been transformed into a domain of theft and hatred, contrary to its intended status as a house of prayer. During the Mass, other speakers recount familiar actions by the occupying forces aimed at expelling Palestinians from the land: revoking residential permits, seizing land for settlements and the Wall, uprooting trees, isolating the West Bank from East Jerusalem, and inducing economic hardship. As if to underscore the bond with the land and its people, AEI's Bethlehem Sumud Choir is attired in traditional clothing, singing of the Lord's blessings upon the earth.

I recollect how this region used to be an excellent hiking destination years ago. One could journey not only to Cremisan but also to Walajeh, facing encirclement by the Wall, to the Jerusalem zoo, and the British Mandate-era railroad at the verdant village of Battir nearby. Like Cremisan and other villages in the vicinity, Battir is imperiled by Wall construction. A proposal to designate the village a World Heritage Site is underway to

The Birthplace of Jesus Is in Palestine

safeguard it from Wall encroachment. To preserve the Palestinian presence on the land, novel and imaginative actions must be conceived, challenging the world's complicity while asserting both a physical and moral presence.

※

Rev. Saliba stands at an improvised open-air altar, offering prayers and speaking resolutely while Israeli soldiers observe behind him, accompanied by a military jeep. His demeanor is calm, but his words are forceful: "Here it happens that land, trees, and people are destroyed."

On Wednesday, September 2, 2015, we gather with a German Pax Christi group from Augsburg at the base of an imposing high bridge in Beit Jala. This bridge serves Israeli settlers commuting between Jerusalem and the Hebron and Gush Etzion settlements, a road partly inaccessible to Palestinians from the West Bank. In the valley below lies the village of Bir 'Ona, a neighborhood grappling with an unfathomable legal and political status.

On one hand, its land has been annexed by Israel to Jerusalem, and some of its families hold Jerusalem IDs, at least until now. On the other hand, the village is situated in the West Bank, prompting inhabitants to occasionally apply for permits to access Jerusalem. Historically, Bir 'Ona has been linked with the town of Beit Jala.

Residents have long sought clarity on their status, particularly to determine how they can legally construct homes that are presently often subjected to demolition. However, the outcome is that life becomes increasingly untenable, a silent ethnic cleansing in progress.

Over 100 ancient olive trees across from the houses are razed to make space for the Wall in this valley leading to Cremisan. In the Cremisan area, fifty-eight Palestinian families are losing access to their lands, which is expected to be located beyond the Wall, all under the pretext of security concerns.

The daily prayer service occurs amidst the cacophony of a bulldozer and the droning of the jeep. At times, the reverend's own words are drowned out. From a lofty rooftop, soldiers observe the scene.

Rev. Rishmawi receives support from the local parish priest, Akhtam Hijazin. He shares that the soldiers claim to be here for our protection. "Of course, they protect themselves," he adds. "Why is it necessary for Israel to occupy not only the hilltops [settlements on Beit Jala lands], the tunnels through the hills, and the bridges between the hills, but also the valley?"

The outcome, according to Saliba, is that people are leaving. Not only the youth but also families. Just last week, seven families departed Beit Jala for Europe and the US. A sense of powerlessness hangs over the gathering. Fuad, the Institute's founder, is present; his eye is red due to tear gas fired during the service on Sunday. His daughter Rania, the Institute's director, cannot attend due to lingering headaches from the same Sunday incident.

Guided by the clarinet's melody, we sing "We Shall Overcome" in response to the surrounding noise. Afterward, I walk back with a colleague who shares an encounter from Sunday. A female Israeli soldier approached him in Hebrew, to which he didn't respond due to his lack of fluency in the language. A male soldier then approached, questioning his lack of "respectful" interaction with the female soldier and warning him that he would be arrested if such a situation occurred again.

☙

It is January 2021. Mary and I decide to explore the area surrounding our new apartment in Beit Jala. Taking a taxi to Cremisan Monastery, we find solace in this quiet and forested haven. As we gaze into a valley, with Israeli settlements perched high on the opposite side, our taxi driver remarks that despite its natural beauty, he wouldn't want to live there. Two Palestinian houses in the valley require the presence of soldiers to open the gate in front of their homes.

An annual card grants access to Cremisan. While walking along the paths, we encounter numerous individuals walking, sitting, and jogging; a rather unusual sight in Palestine. Even a car with bicycles mounted on top passes by. Mary captures the blooming almond trees in full blossom through her camera lens, sighing at the beauty while recognizing the highly limited mobility of Palestinians, even beyond the constraints of the pandemic.

On our return journey, a fence protected by coiled barbed wire comes into view. Behind it lies a new, yet unused road that halts just fifty meters from the road leading to Cremisan. I wonder if this is a Palestinian road, but the realization dawns upon me that it's an Israeli road leading to Road 60, the route used by settlers heading south in the West Bank. I recall the ceremonial protest against the Wall's construction years ago, where a glimpse of this new road was inadvertently witnessed. It becomes clear that those aiming to visit Cremisan in the future will be directed through this road. The monastery is slated to be integrated into "Greater Jerusalem."

Perhaps we can still use our annual entry card to Cremisan this year, I ponder. However, I anticipate that the geopolitical landscape will worsen, depending on the decisions of Israeli authorities and judges. Walking or jogging through these paths may become restricted. Since moving here in the 1990s, I've sensed that Israel isn't merely constructing roads and settlements, but also shaping international public opinion, particularly during publicity moments like those involving Cremisan. Initial waves of indignation and protest tend to fade, and the plans are eventually carried out. Is Cremisan a lost cause? Mary suggests that Biden might be able to intervene, but I believe that sustained cultural protests alongside sites of apartheid hold value, especially when combined with the power of social media.

As we make our way back, we observe the rising of many new apartment buildings, some of which appear as unfinished structures. The old charm of Beit Jala is gradually fading, yet remnants of its past glory persist in the form of aged houses adorned with images of St George on their lintels. Yellow Israeli license plates are a common sight, indicating individuals relocating from Jerusalem to the Bethlehem district, likely driven by the high rents in the former.

Amidst the changing landscape, some businesses have shuttered, while others like pet shops seem to flourish in these times of the pandemic. A lone flower shop remains open, perhaps offering a source of solace for clients seeking a bit of comfort.

※

Spring of 2022 arrives.

The Palestinian Right to Movement organization is making commendable efforts, linking the liberation of the country with the liberation of the environment. During a walk to Cremisan, we encounter well-placed signs along the road to the gate, urging visitors to maintain cleanliness in the area. The slogans include messages like: "Cleanliness is from faith, dirt is from you" and "Instead of garbage, let us breathe freedom."

The eighth Palestine Marathon takes place after a two-year hiatus due to the pandemic. With around ten thousand participants spanning four tracks, including a full forty-two kilometer race, a twenty-one kilometer race, a ten kilometer race, and a five kilometer family run, the event gathers over seventy nationalities, including consulate staff from Jerusalem. Unsurprisingly, the theme is freedom of movement. Facing people complaining about road closures, Mary explains to someone that a marathon once a year shouldn't pose a significant inconvenience.

The marathon serves as a form of resisting presence, particularly when its route intersects with the Wall.

I venture to a barber shop and cross the Hebron Road, where runners are making their way. A band plays traditional Palestinian music, a *dabkeh* group performs elsewhere, and scouts distribute water bottles. An atmosphere of relaxation prevails.

The air in the barber shop is filled with smoke, with everyone except me and the customer in the chair smoking. A man walks in to retrieve a cup of coffee, shares his thoughts on the haircut, and returns with a cigarette, placing it between the lips of the customer. Another person lights it up.

Conversations flow, touching on topics such as street closures, upcoming municipal elections, and the recent increase in wheat and fuel prices. Bethlehem's bakeries had recently gone on strike due to flour prices, but it seems a new supply is expected from Russia at the end of the month. A barber recommends a shop with more affordable prices.

There's an increased focus on walks and runs these days. Right to Movement and Amos Trust organize a "Run the Wall" event, a global run covering 750 km against the Wall. Anyone can contribute kilometers to the cause, and donations support the rebuilding of destroyed homes.

While sumud is often associated with staying put, it could become immobile if it remains primarily defensive and protective. While the idea of sumud, rooted in peasant culture, might risk being inflexible, the Right to Movement organization underscores the importance of movement.

By February of the following year, I find myself recovering from surgery in a Beit Jala hospital room. From my window, I can glimpse the distant Cremisan Monastery. After a heavy rainfall, a rainbow forms an umbrella-like arc over the landscape. Meanwhile, Israeli bulldozers arrive to demolish a house near the hospital in the path of the new small settler road leading from Jerusalem to Cremisan.

13

The Hellish Road

TAKING A TAXI FROM Bethlehem to Ramallah via Wadi Nar proves to be quite an adventure. The journey feels akin to being inside a washing machine, as the winding road on the east side of Jerusalem, known as Wadi Nar or "valley of fire" (or "hell"), twists and turns through the landscape. This road is commonly used by Palestinians to travel between the southern and northern parts of the West Bank. The experience is a blend of being pushed from side to side and up and down due to the road's winding nature, as well as the presence of small "hills" created by residents living along the road. The hills are constructed to slow down traffic. They ensure the safety of people, particularly school children walking along the road. The hill-building initiative took place during the late 1980s, during the first Intifada, when Palestinian police were on strike and speeding cars were a concern. As time passed, various sections of the road were upgraded and widened, often with funding from international organizations such as USAID.

While foreigners might appreciate the road's sneaky twists for the stunning desert views they offer to the east, locals hold a different sentiment due to the road's steep cliffs and perilous drops. For those unable to travel north through Jerusalem, taking the Wadi Nar route becomes a necessity; whether in their own car, although some drivers prefer to avoid it, or via taxi. Wadi Nar is a road used to bypass Jerusalem from the east, leading to the "container checkpoint," a notorious bottleneck between Bethlehem and Ramallah. After this checkpoint, various road options open up, none of which are particularly satisfying. When bypassing Jerusalem on the east, taxi drivers experiment with different routes, sometimes opting

The Hellish Road

for newly constructed settlement roads, while other times avoiding narrow, older streets that can quickly become congested with traffic.

The increasing number of cars on West Bank roads is causing congestion issues on roadways that were never designed to accommodate such volumes. Occasionally, mobile Israeli checkpoints appear, prompting drivers to warn each other about which roads to avoid.

Among drivers, Wadi Nar is known as the road that eats your nerves due to its unpredictable nature. You can never predict what's going to happen next along this route.

Traveling through Wadi Nar can be a relatively quick experience, or it can lead to getting stuck in seemingly hopeless traffic jams. The road's challenging conditions have contributed to numerous accidents, exacerbated by the fact that Palestinian police struggle to effectively enforce traffic regulations along many stretches. The road's poor maintenance, U-turns, and reckless driving further contribute to its hazards. Vulnerable groups such as children, school students, the elderly, and individuals with disabilities are particularly at risk along this route.

By its unpredictability, Wadi Nar reflects the intricate network of roads in the West Bank that Palestinians navigate every day.

※

During the Byzantine era, the monk Theodosios founded a monastery near the road that is believed to be the path taken by the three wise men to avoid revealing the birthplace of Jesus to the authorities in Jerusalem. The monastery, with only one monk remaining, still stands at this location. Further east, at the end of a road in the valley, lies the impressive Mar Saba Monastery, home to more monks. This monastery serves as a reminder of the time when monks sought to emulate Jesus by testing themselves in the depths of the desert. According to a tale shared with a Scottish author, a Greek monk at Mar Saba mentioned with a degree of satisfaction that on the Day of Judgment, the corpses of sinners would flow from the Kidron valley along the monastery to the lifeless Dead Sea.

On a school excursion in 2000, around a hundred students and teachers visited Mar Saba. Since women are not allowed to enter the monastery, teacher-storyteller Suzy engaged the girls outside the building by narrating legends about Wadi Nar. Among the many stories about the caves in Wadi Nar, one adaptation from the Brothers Grimm stands out. In this tale, the Angel of Death had chosen a cave along the treacherous road. When a chance visitor stumbled upon the cave, he saw an immense chamber illuminated by candles of varying lengths, some nearly extinguished. The visitor inquired about these candles, and the Angel explained that each represented a person's life, extinguishing upon their death. When the visitor asked about his own candle, the Angel gestured casually toward a small, low-burning flame. In his anxiety, the visitor knocked his candle to the ground, and died there instantly. The Angel remarked that altering one's life's course comes with consequences.

⁓

In my notes of February 5-12, 2001, an acquaintance who lectures at Bethlehem University's English Department shares his frustration about his weekly Saturday commute to Al-Najah University in Nablus, located in the northern part of the West Bank. The journey, normally two and a half hours, has extended to three and a half hours due to road conditions. He describes the experience as a blend of the "hellish Wadi Nar road along the east of Jerusalem and a northern road that resembles something out of Alice in Wonderland—riddled with challenges but devoid of the expected enjoyment."

Personal memories of the Wadi Nar road also resurface. At the beginning of my stay in Palestine during an evening journey in heavy rain, I found myself in a taxi filled with passengers, navigating the road's twists and turns as it climbed hills. During this journey, the melody of The Beatles' "The Long and Winding Road" entered my mind, becoming a metaphor for my personal experience of the country and our financial struggles at the time. Since then, the melody of that Beatles song has forever been associated with the road.

⁓

In 2002 during the second Intifada, while on the way back from Ramallah to Bethlehem under curfew, I take a longer route through the far eastern outskirts of Jerusalem with some young workers who are breaking the curfew to illegally work in Jerusalem. The desert road becomes blocked at one point, leading us to climb down a rocky hill and walk for half an hour. This unexpected walk takes us through Wadi Nar. As we descend to the small

The Hellish Road

Kidron "river," which is unfortunately a polluted sewage stream due to the negligence of the Jerusalem municipality, we encounter a checkpoint where several vans are waiting. These drivers are attempting to navigate the checkpoint, but tensions arise as they debate who would give me a ride. Eventually, one car agrees to take us deep into Bethlehem despite the curfew. The car's main door cannot close properly, but the workers and I are undeterred by such details. The workers share their dreams of visiting "Amsterdam," with one making an obscene gesture. When asked if they can come to Amsterdam, I respond with *"yareet"* (hopefully), always a useful phrase.

However, our journey takes an unexpected turn when the driver suddenly stops behind a parked car and makes a frantic wave with his hand. The situation seems dire as we appear stranded. An armored personnel carrier and a new checkpoint are set up. The workers attempt to pass through the checkpoint but are denied access and forced to turn back. As a foreign passport holder, I am able to enter the curfewed area. Walking approximately a kilometer into Beit Sahour, I hail a passing car, which turns out to be the same van carrying the same passengers. They have managed to find a short detour and joyfully invite me to join them once again. They leave the van near 'Azza camp and continue on foot, becoming six shadows walking through the eerily quiet streets of Bethlehem.

※

In 2001, Mary shares an incident involving the Wadi Nar road. She tells me that settlers are currently waving Palestinian flags on the road to attract the attention of taxi drivers who take dirt roads. However, when the taxis follow the direction indicated by the flags, the settlers open fire on them.

A story collected by the Institute during the second Intifada adds another layer to the account. The story tells of a man who used to travel to Jerusalem for work but is compelled to take the Wadi Nar bypass road due to the numerous checkpoints and permit issues. With mobile checkpoints often present on this route, the man and his friend find themselves escaping Israeli soldiers by crawling through an underground drainage system. They manage to reach their workplaces safely.

The Birthplace of Jesus Is in Palestine

❧

In 2011, tragedy strikes as a bus carrying kindergarten children collides with a truck north of the Wadi Nar road, resulting in the deaths of 9 young children and a teacher. Mary had a premonition that morning as she thought about the hazardous road conditions during the winter rains, the accidents that frequently occur, and the inadequately paved roads. She reflected on the accidents that often happen on the bypass road that people are forced to take due to the situation. The accident takes place north of Jerusalem, not far from a checkpoint. The news devastates Mary, who lies defeated on her bed, crying for the young lives lost. It's revealed that two girls had embraced each other in their final moments. The parents receive delayed information, with some initially believing their children had died, only to find out later that they were still alive. A terrible image emerges of a child only being identified by the key to the home worn around her neck.

❧

In December 2019, amid escalating attacks against settlers and subsequent Israeli army actions, it's reported that people in Bethlehem and Ramallah have begun opening their doors to travelers stranded on the Wadi Nar road. This gesture of offering accommodation to those afraid to venture out at night on the highway due to potential attacks by settlers highlights the tense atmosphere in the area. Reports indicate that after a Palestinian attack on settlers, there were numerous incidents of stone-throwing against Palestinian cars within twenty-four hours.

Reflecting on the past year, I acknowledge the challenges faced by Palestinian life and politics. However, amidst the difficulties, there are also a few bright spots to be found. I note the Institute's involvement in "sumud advocacy" projects in West Bank schools in 2019. These projects aim to encourage teenagers to strengthen their society and develop leadership skills to address conflicts in their environment. One particularly notable project takes place in a school in 'Abediyyeh, a village on the east side of Bethlehem. The students choose "Wadi Nar" as their conflict theme, focusing on the container checkpoint. This checkpoint is notorious for its difficulties, and the students are particularly shocked by a soldier taking a selfie with a long line of waiting cars, demonstrating the power dynamics at play.

At one school, students manage to accelerate the construction of a road that would make their journey to school safer. Recognizing the dangerous conditions posed by the Wadi Nar road, they organize efforts to improve the situation. Police officers and local officials now guide students crossing the road near the school, and an ambulance has become available for emergencies.

Similarly, at another school in the village of Dar Salah, students collaborate to address the risks associated with the road. They organize morning buses to transport them to a nearby checkpoint, reducing the need for students to walk along the dangerous road. Parents, medical committees, and drivers are involved in efforts to enhance safety and minimize risks.

Still another school engaged in the conflict project focuses on haphazard apartment block development, using examples from urban quarters, especially the town of Doha, south of Bethlehem. This expansion is fueled in part by Palestinians seeking refuge in such quarters due to economic pressures in East Jerusalem. The school recognizes that this migration from one conflict zone to another places significant strain on services and facilities. With the guidance of their teachers, students obtain a promise from the city council to restrict building heights to four levels to prevent excessive pressure on services. The students take pride in their achievements and are determined to hold local authorities accountable.

The success of the students' initiatives can be attributed to a combination of factors. The timing of their actions and the pressing nature of their concerns likely play a role. The significant number of students involved, representing extended families, give their demands a broad community backing that the municipality cannot ignore. The students' non-political stance allows them to raise questions that others might hesitate to ask, and the support of the Ministry of Education lends credibility to their efforts. Enthusiastic teachers, school heads, and inspectors contribute to their success.

However, their successes are achieved within an extremely problematic context. The Palestinian police, as a representative of the Palestinian Authority, faces credibility issues due to ongoing political struggles. The overarching occupation of the West Bank creates an environment of insecurity and lawlessness, particularly in areas under Israeli control, where settlers and criminal elements exploit the situation.

The challenges related to public space and infrastructure planning in the West Bank reflect the complex governance dynamics in the region. Local municipalities and Palestinian authorities face limitations in their ability to plan and execute public works, particularly in areas near traditional city boundaries or areas under different levels of Israeli control (areas B and C). The absence of a comprehensive local-regional master plan and the constraints on decision-making authority hinder the implementation of larger infrastructure projects, leaving much of the Palestinian traffic network and public works underdeveloped. The increase in the number of cars in urban areas like Bethlehem adds to congestion and frustration.

In contrast, modern highways primarily connecting Israeli settlements and settlements with Jerusalem often serve as efficient transportation routes, further highlighting the disparities in infrastructure development between different areas in the West Bank.

14

Common Home

> "Sumud is the discovery of my roots, living this rootedness in this land, and living the will to love one's neighbor in all its aspects. This all is part of my Christianity."[1]
>
> —Munther Isaac, Academic Dean at the Bethlehem Bible College, and Christ at the Checkpoint Conference

JUNE 2016: I AM currently assisting in the editing of a book[2] featuring stories from Palestinian school students on Muslim-Christian living together. This project is part of a long-running initiative by AEI, led by its coordinator Fuad Giacaman, which is focused on "preventive education." Its aim is to thwart the abduction of Muslim-Christian relations by fear, prejudice, and exclusive policies.

Across thirty schools in the Bethlehem and Ramallah districts, Christian and Muslim students engage in joint religious education sessions, which typically occur separately, a few times per month or semester. These joint sessions intend to foster a deeper understanding of each other's religions and to cultivate mutual respect. Palestine has a rich history of interreligious living together, which sometimes faces strain, among other things due to the Israeli occupation causing potential divides between Muslims

---

1. Interview Munther Isaac by AEI-Pax Christi/Fuad Giacaman and Roger Salameh, Bethlehem, October 2020.
2. Giacaman, *Hand in Hand*.

and Christians. Additionally, the emergence of *Daesh* (ISIS) and repressive practices in neighboring countries has added challenges. As part of the project, students aged fourteen to seventeen are tasked with collecting and documenting inspiring stories about Muslim-Christian living together.

What's particularly striking in these narratives is the power of human gestures. Arab hospitality has a long tradition of generous gestures, with timely, spontaneous actions being highly valued in Arab culture. Often, these gestures are acts of support during times of need. One Muslim woman recounts an incident at a primary school in Nablus when she lent five shekels to her Christian classmate Therese, who couldn't afford the bus fare home. This act of kindness blossomed into a lifelong friendship. Years later, in a remarkable turn, Therese selflessly donated her kidney to save the Muslim woman's life, though the medical intervention ultimately led to Therese's passing due to side effects.

Decades prior to the Nakba, two children from neighboring Muslim and Christian families in Lydda (in Hebrew: Lod) grew up together. In 1948, both Mohammed and Tony, along with their families, sought refuge in Syria due to conflict. When Tony, now in his seventies, faced a threat from a *Daesh* soldier, Mohammed valiantly shielded him, resulting in the tragic loss of both their lives. Many other accounts describe how Muslim and Christian families supported each other amidst Intifadas and political oppression.

There are also captivating stories of adhering to customs or practices of the other religion. In the streets of Ramallah, Palestinian-Christian youths distributed water and dates just before the fast-breaking during Ramadan. On another occasion, when an imam fell ill, the church bells tolled to signal the end of fasting. Similarly, a Christian man assumed the role of *mousharater*, awakening Muslim believers for an early breakfast before fasting commenced.

Christian families and a church pooled resources to sponsor needy and devout Muslims on their pilgrimage to Mecca. Muslims also participated in the reconstruction of a church severely damaged after an attack by occupying forces. Instances of interfaith goodwill extend beyond Palestine, as evidenced by Jordanians naming a new mosque in Madaba after 'Issa, or Jesus, as a gesture of solidarity with Christians.

In reality, the Middle East is replete with such instances of goodwill that often fade amidst present tensions. Documenting and disseminating these stories serves the cause of inclusive education and the celebration of human bonds across religious lines.

Sometimes, people wonder: Why focus so much on Islam and Christianity? Why not simply discuss human solidarity or human civic behavior instead of interreligious living together? With media constantly magnifying ongoing associations, Islam and Christianity are often portrayed as opposing forces in the public perception. The discourse about "Islamic" and "Christian" Palestinians, some argue, further divides Palestinians, even though this division is not as pronounced as in other parts of the Middle East.

Yet, it's important to continue discussing the everyday aspects of Islam and Christianity, which are integral to the diverse tapestry of normal life. Amidst the occasional tensions and differences, living together across religious lines brings a unique richness, though this sentiment might sound idealistic in today's world.

In a way, human gestures are the essence of life, etched into memory. I hold dear those instances where even strangers willingly give their full and immediate attention in a split second. Such occurrences, I find, aren't unusual here. Altruist and political activist Simone Weil once stated that "attention is the rarest and purest form of generosity."[3]

Perhaps the most unusual gesture I encountered was near Nativity Square, when a tourist police officer noticed Jara, then a schoolchild in standard school uniform, receiving some shekels from me for a drink. The police officer assumed Jara, who appeared Palestinian, was begging me, a presumed tourist. With a determined action, he returned the shekels to me and instead gave Jara some money himself, in a friendly attempt to teach her the lesson of not begging. It took Jara and me a while to grasp what had happened.

Of course, one could argue that some form of interest underlies each gesture.

But is that truly an issue? Gestures are woven into the social fabric that sustains daily life. They're about those small, intricate elements that collectively form the human household. It's imperative not to exclude anyone from this communal dwelling. Gestures are also part of human sumud. In fact, my colleague Rania once said that sumud for her represents "life on earth," and that she prefers positive, "giving" or "joy" approaches to sumud over the idea that sumud is only or primarily sacrifice. Without

---

3. The citation is from: Weil, *The Need for Roots*. See: https://www.goodreads.com/quotes/522585-attention-is-the-rarest-and-purest-form-of-generosity

The Birthplace of Jesus Is in Palestine

the individual pearls of gestures, grander projects and concepts hold little meaning or chance of success.

FIGURE 9

Child in front of the Wall in north Bethlehem

15

Sumud and Hope

It is October 2015. The passing of Mary's sister Janet brings a mix of emotions, ranging from sadness and despair to a sense of community and hope. Janet's sudden decease is a shock to the family, and her loss is deeply felt. She was a beloved presence in the household, playing a significant role in nurturing the family and acting as a second mother to the children. The open coffin in the family holds Janet's peaceful corpse, and family members gather to offer prayers and pay their respects.

Despite the somber occasion, life continues around them, with shooting sounds from nearby Rachel's Tomb serving as a stark reminder of the ongoing conflict. The memorial service takes place in the Church of the Nativity, where poignant moments like the family's final kisses on Janet's face before the coffin is closed are particularly touching.

The days of mourning reflect the transformation from initial silent sadness to a more animated communal atmosphere. The community comes together to support one another, and conversations become livelier as people engage with each other. Even though tears are always close at hand, the shared experience helps the family and community to come alive again after the loss.

This sense of community is palpable in Palestinian culture, where cafeterias at schools and universities are vibrant spaces for social interaction. Despite the challenges and the frequent presence of sorrow, there remains a strong undercurrent of hope and resilience among the people.

The Birthplace of Jesus Is in Palestine

Indian writer Arundhati Roy's words once written on the Wall at Rachel's Tomb, "Another world is not only possible, she is on her way. On a quiet day I can hear her breathing," resonate as a beacon of hope. This phrase is a strong reminder that hope is not an abstract notion of a distant future, but a tangible and rhythmic force that embodies the essence of life. The breath symbolizes the spirit of life and the promise of renewal. It stands in contrast to the suffocation in Palestine caused by daily violence, humiliation, and a lack of dignity.

Hope is found in the simple things, as reflected in Mahmoud Darwish's writings.

> We have an incurable malady: hope. Hope in liberation and independence. Hope in a normal life where we are neither heroes nor victims. Hope that our children will go safely to their schools. Hope that a pregnant woman will give birth to a living baby at the hospital, and not a dead child in front of a military checkpoint; hope that our poets will see the beauty of the colour red in roses rather than in blood; hope that this land will take up its original name: the land of love and peace.[1]

Even in the face of despair, it's necessary to invent and create hope. Darwish stresses the importance of finding hope in the beauty of nature, the beauty of life, and the fragility that comes with it. This notion of hope is not detached from reality, but rooted in the fundamental aspects of existence.

Amid challenges and turmoil, the yearning for hope and the belief in a better future remain central to the strength of the Palestinian people.

The approach to hope from a citizen's perspective, as presently articulated by a scholar and activist such as Rebecca Solnit, emphasizes the importance of reality-based hope that allows for uncertainty and potentiality.[2] This form of hope is not synonymous with either absolute pessimism or naive optimism. It's grounded in a radical non-acceptance of the present and a belief in change through collective social efforts driven by the nonviolent power of citizens. This perspective aligns with the concept of sumud, which is also not a static property but requires activation and struggle to be preserved.

---

1. The quote is mentioned in Saith, "Mahmoud Darwish," 29.
2. Solnit, *Hope in the Dark*.

Sumud and Hope

Paulo Freire's critical pedagogy of hope[3], often cited by Palestinians, highlights the reciprocal relationship between hope and struggle. Hope generates the energy to engage in meaningful struggle, and in turn, struggle generates more hope. This dynamic is also present in sumud. Both hope and sumud imply an ongoing, long-term commitment to a better future, even if the specifics of that future are not fully known.

On a more abstract level, hope and sumud both reflect a belief in the power of human agency to bring about change in the world. They reject the notion of a dead or predetermined world and instead emphasize the changeability of the world through collective energy and action.

In order to mobilize sumud, it's essential to shift perspective and look beyond dominant narratives and superficial media accounts. Instead, we should focus on the stories, experiences, and struggles of common people at the margins. These unexplored sources of hope and sumud often emerge from community-based efforts and places. Whether rooted in the familiar rhythms of home or in the shadow of adversity, hope and sumud exist side by side, reflecting the determination of people in the face of challenges.

Active collective memory plays a crucial role in both hope and sumud, providing a foundation for hopeful actions. Memory activism involves actively engaging with the past, whether it's through reconnecting with landscapes where Palestinian homes once stood or resisting attempts to erase historical narratives. Community joy, a form of collective celebration, also contributes to sustaining hope and sumud. The outbursts of joy following positive events, such as Palestinian singers winning contests, serve as expressions of hope.

Hope adds an imaginative and prophetic dimension to sumud, enabling moral imagination to flourish. This imaginative capacity is supported by creative forms like dreams, prayers, wishes, graffiti, songs, and poetry. Artists, in their role as "hopetellers" (Brueggemann), contribute to nurturing this aspect of hope. Playful and game-like genres, often associated with children's life, have the ability to break through the constraints of a suffering reality, offering fresh perspectives and alternative ways of looking at the world. Hope is transformative in nature, and it can inspire and inform the practice of sumud.

At the core of hope is a belief, sometimes naive but deeply powerful, that the struggle for humanity and life itself is always worthwhile. This

---

3. Freire, *Pedagogy*.

belief provides a profound source of energy for continued engagement with the challenges of life, even in the face of immense obstacles.

※

I think that the concept of "small victories" is central to both sumud and hope in the Palestinian context. Similar to hope, sumud is not solely based on enduring and continuous struggle, but it also involves an active form of "waiting" that seeks out small first steps or achievements that serve as signposts of hope. These small victories, whether material or psychological, serve as building blocks that collectively contribute to larger victories. These victories can be both tangible and intangible, ranging from concrete milestones to internal changes in attitude or behavior.

Small victories have a unifying effect on the community, fostering solidarity and volunteerism. They represent moral achievements that strengthen the bonds within the community and create a shared sense of purpose. This sense of unity and shared energy amplifies the impact of these small victories, creating a momentum that can inspire larger victories and transformative change.

In the face of Israeli military control and policies aimed at stifling hope and resistance, Palestinians continue to strive for these small victories. The Israeli army employs bureaucratic hurdles, intimidation tactics, and violence to create a sense of predictability and control over the occupation. The modern tools of control, such as checkpoints and surveillance techniques, are designed to create a sense of despair. The strategy is to discourage Palestinians from challenging Israeli policies by fostering a perception that resistance only leads to worsened conditions.

Yet, Palestinians have managed to find ways to resist, organize, and plant the seeds of change in their collective memory. The struggle against the construction of the Wall in villages like Bil'in demonstrates how small local victories, even when only temporary, can have a lasting impact on people's minds and contribute to the broader struggle.

Storytelling plays a critical role in preserving both hope and sumud in the Palestinian context. The struggle for control over narratives is a central aspect of conflicts, where different parties seek to establish legitimacy and sway public opinion through the stories they tell.

The basic story grammar of struggle that underlies both sumud and hope aligns with the human experience of seeking courage and envisioning a different future. Confronted with humiliation and dehumanization, those Palestinians who recount their experiences engage in a form of narrative meaning-making that reshapes perspectives between storytellers and their audience. Even in seemingly futile situations, Palestinians continue to take action, whether individual or collective, and these actions themselves become stories that can inspire hope. Indeed, stories reveal the proximity of hope and hopelessness, portraying life's unpredictable realities where promise and danger, vulnerability and inner strength, beauty and tragedy, goodness and cruelty, resilience and fragility, coexist and intersect.

The prophetic genres mentioned in this book—prayers, songs—and the significance of young and older generations documenting their experiences, preserving a collective memory through cultural exhibitions, singing next to the Wall, oral history initiatives, or a wall museum, embody hopeful acts. Sharing the practices of sumud with a broader international audience allows for a more humane portrayal of Palestinian reality, dismantling the familiar stereotypes that have taken hold.

The envisioning and enactment of new narratives can transform the perception of reality. An illustration of this is the imaginative reconfiguration of spaces, such as viewing checkpoints as places of prayer (as once proposed by Mgr Michel Sabbah) or as places of learning, or the creative reinterpretation of the Wall as a stage, canvas, or obstacle to be surmounted. This process challenges conventional readings of the world, inviting a fresh perspective that uncovers potentially emancipating stories. These evocative and inspiring tales can be shared through various mediums, including various media platforms.

Social movements thrive on storytelling as a means of defining their identity, introducing their goals, and communicating their victories. By sharing stories of especially small victories, movements can accumulate momentum and foster transformative change. The communication of stories of sumud, in particular, offers a strategy for building up a record of lived experiences that may not feature prominently in official historical narratives but are nonetheless powerful in their impact on individuals and communities.

Afterword: Bethlehem, Christmas 2023

THE MASSACRE BY HAMAS on October 7 in south Israel led to an invasion of Gaza by the Israeli army in which at the time of writing—end December 2023—over 21.000 Gazans were killed, and a multiple number of persons injured and handicapped.

Besan was a Palestinian third-year student of medicine in Gaza. The bombings by the Israeli army killed her mid-October together with 12 members of her family. Besan's last post on X (formerly Twitter): "I have dreams I have not yet fulfilled," she wrote. "I have a life that I have not fully lived." "I have a family that I love and fear for," she continued. "If we are all exterminated by this barbaric occupation, our crime is simply that one day we defended our land that was stolen from us and demanded our basic rights as human beings. We will not forgive the whole world."[1]

Just before she died, she also wrote on Facebook: "When I talk with people here (. . .) they don't want to be called heroes. They didn't ask to be heroes, they just asked to live. And they're asking for a ceasefire now." And: "Constantly being fed this narrative of the Gazans' resilience and strength against [the] oppression, the apartheid and the occupation, when we cannot and will never cope with the violence. Calling us resilient just frees the world from responsibility and guilt (. . .)."[2]

Her last words oblige one to take a pause, certainly so in a book reflecting on sumud. The meaning of sumud, as well as comparable concepts like resilience, hope or resistance, can become hollow and perverted when they create impossible demands while taking away other people's responsibility to affect a real change in an inhuman situation like in Gaza. It is in

---

1. Quoted in *The Independent*: Davis, "Haunting Last Message."
2. https://www.facebook.com/p/Besan-H-Helasa-100015031876972/

itself true that many people in Gaza have shown in the last months of 2023 enormous strength, determination and improvisational ability. However, they have been in the first place victims asking for immediate and practical support in their struggle for survival.

During previous wars sumud meant for Palestinians to stay on the land, if at all possible. In the war in Gaza sumud got an additional, disturbing layer of meaning, namely, people being trapped in the open air prison of Gaza against their will. "We remain steadfast in spite of ourselves," people said according to *Haaretz* journalist Amira Hass.[3]

The neighboring Arab country, Egypt, and other Arab countries have been clear in their refusal to accept Palestinian refugees from Gaza, for their own reasons. But nothing is sure, as right-wing nationalist circles in Israel, present in its government, are having an agenda of ethnic cleansing while some plan for the return of new Israeli settlements in Gaza, after these were withdrawn in 2005.

Almost all Palestinians in Gaza, nearly 2,3 million, were forced to flee in the tiny strip from one place to another. Half October, still before the Israeli ground invasion, some Palestinians who fled from north Gaza to the south thought they would rather go back to their homes as south Gaza turned out also not to be safe. They preferred to die at home. It is important to remember that Gaza's population are mostly refugees from 1948, and some refused to flee a second time, having lost their original homes in what became Israel seventy-five years ago.

A key meaning of sumud is holding to a home where one belongs. But as a home the future of Gaza is bleak. What happened in the war has been described by some commentators as *domicide*, that is, the destruction of people's homes on a massive scale. There is almost no societal infrastructure anymore in Gaza, many of the schools, hospitals, hotels, mosques, churches, graveyards, libraries, museums, and other cultural and social places, with all the people who lived and worked there, have been heavily damaged or totally vanished. Moreover, following declarations by the Israeli leadership, it is very possible that the Palestinians in Gaza will after the war come under direct Israeli occupation for a prolonged time.

The Palestinian home is also severely disrupted in the West Bank. In the shadow of Gaza, the West Bank has become a potential new front, with an intensification of processes of colonization and Nakba, or forced

---

3. Hass, "Gazan Dilemma."

Afterword: Bethlehem, Christmas 2023

displacement. Hundreds of Palestinians have been killed during the massive raids by the Israeli army into the West Bank cities, which have furthermore been badly damaged by the incursions. According to inhabitants, the Jenin refugee camp in the north of the West Bank has turned into a "little Gaza." Israeli settlers expelled the inhabitants of over a dozen shepherd communities in the southern Hebron hills from their lands. In areas near Ramallah and Jericho and in the northern Jordan Valley many Bedouin families were forced to leave their lands for the same reason.

Preventing the possibility of a Palestinian state and annexing the land seems to have become the project of Israeli prime minister Netanyahu and many of the settlers. The Palestinian population has been subjected to a regime of humiliation to an even greater extent than described in this book. It seems that October 7 fundamentally shook Israel's subjective assessment of its capacity to hold the Palestinian population into long-term obedience. Israel's overwhelming display of violence in Gaza has apparently been aimed, at least in part, to restore the so-called "deterrence." The Palestinian willpower and sumud are once again tested to the limit. But also in the West Bank and in Bethlehem sumud has become a term with its own contradictions. When one could look into the hearts of young people here, most likely many would silently wish to be able to emigrate in order to have some kind of future which is them denied here.

The Lutheran Church in Bethlehem created a Nativity scene whereby Jesus is born in Gaza, in the middle of the rubble of a collapsed house. The Christmas December festivities in Bethlehem were all cancelled.

The Birthplace of Jesus Is in Palestine

FIGURE 10

Manger at the Lutheran Church in Bethlehem, Christmas 2023

Recommended Reading

Additional English-Language Readings on Bethlehem

(Not Comprehensive)

Arab Educational Institute-Open Windows. *Bethlehem Community Book*. Bethlehem: Culture and Palestine Series, 2000.

Atallah, Susan, ed. *Your Stories Are My Stories: A Palestinian Oral History Project*. Bethlehem: Terra Sancta/St Joseph School for Girls, Wi'am Conflict Resolution Center, and the Arab Educational Institute, 2001.

Atallah, Susan, ed. *The Wall Cannot Stop Our Stories: A Palestinian Diary Project*. Bethlehem: Terra Sancta/St Joseph School for Girls, 2004.

Blincoe, Nicholas. *Bethlehem: Biography of a Town*. London: Constable, 2017.

Grey, Mary. *The Advent of Peace: A Gospel Journey to Christmas*. London: SPCK, 2011.

Raheb, Mitri, Fred Strickert and Garo Nalbandian. *Bethlehem 2000*. Northampton MA: Interlink, 1998.

Bibliography

Amiry, Suad. *Sharon and My Mother-in-Law: Ramallah Diaries*. New York: Anchor, 2006.
Arab Educational Institute-Pax Christi. *The Sumud Reader: Interviews and Articles from the Arab Educational Institute in Bethlehem*. Bethlehem: Arab Educational Institute, Culture and Palestine Series. https://aeicenter.org/3d-flip-book/2023-the-sumud-reader/, 2023.
———. Resource: Wall Poster Stories. AEI–Pax Christi website, 2023. https://aeicenter.org/wp-content/uploads/2019/10/AEI-2019-resource-wall-posters-all.pdf
Atallah, Susan, ed. *Your Stories Are My Stories: A Palestinian Oral History Project*. Bethlehem: Terra Sancta/St Joseph School for Girls, Wi'am Conflict Resolution Center, and the Arab Educational Institute, 2001.
Atallah, Susan, ed. *The Wall Cannot Stop Our Stories: A Palestinian Diary Project*. Bethlehem: Terra Sancta/St Joseph School for Girls, 2004.
Berger, Yotam and Nir Hasson. "Israel Pushing Plan to Expand Settlement Toward Bethlehem, Isolating West Bank Village." *Haaretz*, 26 June 2018. https://www.haaretz.com/israel-news/2018-06-26/ty-article/.premium/plan-gains-pace-for-israeli-construction-all-the-way-to-west-bank/0000017f-dbfd-df9c-a17f-fffd471e0000
Crowfoot, Grace M.H. and Louise Baldensperger. *From Cedar to Hyssop; A Study in the Folklore of Plants in Palestine*. New York: Sheldon Press, 1932.
Darwish, Mahmoud. *Palestine as Metaphor*. Translated by Amira El-Zein and Carolyn Forché. Ithaca NY: Olive Branch, 2019.
Davis, Barney. "Haunting Last Message of Teenage Trainee Doctor Killed with Family in Israeli Airstrike." *The Independent*, 18 October 2023. https://www.independent.co.uk/news/world/middle-east/gaza-doctor-israel-hamas-war-b2431150.html
Freire, Paulo. *Pedagogy of the Oppressed*. New York: Seabury, 1970.
Giacaman, Fuad, Walid Mustafa and Toine van Teeffelen, eds. *Hand in Hand: Moslem-Christian Encounters in Palestinian Daily Life*. English and Arabic versions. Bethlehem: Arab Educational Institute: Culture and Palestine Series, 2016.
Hass, Amira. "Palestinian Volunteers Help Olive Harvesters in Ways the Palestinian Authority Can't." *Haaretz*, 23 October 2020. https://www.haaretz.com/middle-east-news/palestinians/2021-10-17/ty-article/.highlight/as-olive-harvest-begins-israeli-soldiers-prevent-palestinians-from-reaching-groves/0000017f-f715-d5bd-a17f-f73ff7c80000
———. "A Gazan Dilemma: When Saving Your Life Is Expulsion by Israel." *Haaretz*, 11 December 2023. https://www.haaretz.com/israel-news/2023-12-11/ty-article/.premium/a-gazan-dilemma-when-saving-your-life-is-expulsion-by-

Bibliography

israel/0000018c-58f0-df2f-adac-fefdc40a0000?utm_source=mailchimp&utm_medium=email&utm_content=author-alert&utm_campaign=Amira%20Hass&utm_term=20231211-15:33

Jabra, Jabra Ibrahim. *The Ship*. Translated by Adnan Haydar and Roger Allen. Builder CO: Lynne Rienner, 1985.

Levisson, Chaim. "Israel Has 101 Different Types of Permits Governing Palestinian Movement." *Haaretz* 23 December 2011. https://www.haaretz.com/2011-12-23/ty-article/israel-has-101-different-types-of-permits-governing-palestinian-movement/0000017f-f034-d497-a1ff-f2b439140000

Lorusso, Stefano. "'They reflect Palestinian Character': Arabian Horse-breeding in the West Bank." *The Guardian*, 9 May 2023. https://www.theguardian.com/artanddesign/2023/may/09/they-reflect-palestinian-character-arabian-horse-breeding-in-the-west-bank

Makdisi, Saree, *Palestine Inside Out: An Everyday Occupation*. New York: W. W. Norton & Company, 2008.

Muhawi, Ibrahim and Sharif Kanaana. *Speak, Bird, Speak Again: Palestinian Arab Folktales*. Berkeley and Los Angeles, CA: University of California Press, 1989.

Murra, Rania and Toine van Teeffelen. "The Wall Museum: Palestinian Stories on the Wall in Bethlehem." *Jerusalem Quarterly*, 55 (2013) 93-96.

Peace Now. "KKL-JNF and its Role in Settlement Expansion," *Newsletter*, 2 April 2020. https://peacenow.org.il/en/settler-national-fund-keren-kayemeth-leisraels-acquisition-of-west-bank-land

———. "KKL-JNF is fighting to expel Palestinians from their homes in the Occupied Territories." *Newsletter*, 23 August 2019. https://peacenow.org.il/en/the-jewish-national-fund-against-palestinians-in-al-makhrour

Raheb, Mitri. "Biblical Narrative and Palestinian Identity in Mahmoud Darwish's Writings." Paper presented at Diyar's Seventh International Conference on "Palestinian Identity in Relation to Time and Space." Bethlehem (August 2013) 89-105. https://www.academia.edu/10809546/Biblical_Narrative_and_Palestinian_Identity_in_Mahmoud_Darwishs_Writings

Saith, Ashwani. "Mahmoud Darwish: Hope as Home in the Eye of the Storm." *Isim Review*, 15 (2005) 28-29, p.29. https://hdl.handle.net/1887/16977

Samaana, Mohammed. Israelis Have Destroyed 1 Million Palestinian Olive Trees; This Month, They're at it Again. *Informed Comment*, 10/20/2020. https://www.juancole.com/2020/10/israeli-destroyed-palestinian.html

Shehadeh, Raja. *The Third Way: A Journal of Life in the West Bank*. London: Quartet Books, 1982.

Solnit, Rebecca. *Hope in the Dark: Untold Histories, Wild Possibilities*. Chicago: Haymarket, 2004.

Stephan H. Stephan, "Modern Palestinian Parallels to the Song of Songs," *Journal of Palestine Oriental Society*, 2 (1922) 199-278.

Tamari, Salim. "Lepers, Lunatics and Saints: The Nativist Ethnography of Tawfiq Canaan and his Jerusalem Circle." In: Salim Tamari. *Mountain against the Sea: Essays on Palestinian Society and Culture*. Berkeley and Los Angeles CA: University of California Press, 2010. https://www.palestine-studies.org/en/node/1648411

Van Teeffelen, Toine. "Rachel's Tomb: Counter-spaces in a Military Geography of Oppression." *Jerusalem Quarterly* 87 (2021) 55-72.

Weil, Simone. *The Need for Roots: Prelude to a Declaration of Duties Towards Mankind*. New York: Routledge, 2002.

www.ingramcontent.com/pod-product-compliance
Lightning Source LLC
Chambersburg PA
CBHW071203160426
43196CB00011B/2179